# TO KILL OR BE KILLED

A TRUE CRIME MEMOIR FROM PRISON

## JONI ANKERSON

WILDBLUE
PRESS

WildBluePress.com

TO KILL OR BE KILLED published by:
WILDBLUE PRESS
P.O. Box 102440
Denver, Colorado 80250

ISBN 978-1-952225-22-2 Trade Paperback
ISBN 978-1-952225-23-9 eBook

Cover design © 2020 WildBlue Press. All rights reserved.

Cover design by Villa Designs

Interior Formatting by Elijah Toten
www.totencreative.com

# TO KILL OR
# BE KILLED

# PART 1

# CHAPTER 1: THE BEGINNING OF THE END

And it was over, just two days after his last violent act. Over for him because he lay bleeding and dead in our bed. Over for me because I had put three bullets in his body from his very own gun. It was the same gun that he had always proudly said was ready to go; "just point and shoot." Indeed, it had worked exactly like he promised. I pointed it at him as he lay asleep and I shot him.

Obviously, I knew better than to take a life — but that was before. Before him. Before he so blatantly and purposefully decided to use me, control me, dominate me, demean me, target me, intimidate me, shame me, guilt me, belittle me, isolate me, manipulate me, diminish me, disrespect me, degrade me, stalk me, rape me, scar and bruise me as a person, make me live in fear, and insist I become a whore and feel like a whore.

When I met him, I had no idea that his attractive qualities and benefits were intentionally luring me into an ugly, sticky web of abuse. It began slowly, of course, and presented itself very innocently and inconspicuously, but over the years it would play out in the ultimate form of power, control, and authority — full-on domestic violence. Hindsight is 20/20, and for me, a painful procedure. But I realize now, 17 years later, after the trauma and tragedy, that I was completely taken advantage of and preyed upon by a master manipulator, abuser, and outright psychopath.

How did this happen? Confidence and positivity were instilled in me by my loving parents from birth and reinforced throughout my entire life. I grew up in a loving and supportive home, with both parents teaching me, my brother, and my two sisters important life lessons of morals, manners, values, and respect. Most importantly, over and above these values to assist in the navigation of my life, was the gift of belief and confidence in myself and my abilities. My parents taught me that I could do anything I set my mind to, and that with hard work and persistence anything was possible. Carrying these lessons throughout the years of growing up and building relationships made it easy to see the good in people. Love and trust came easily, resulting in solid, life-long unions.

But here I am, writing this book from my prison room. I have been in this Michigan prison, the only prison for women in the entire state, for over six years. This fact is important for you to know at this early point for a couple of reasons: the first being that it is, of course, a huge part of my story. But it is also because after these six years in prison, I have finally settled down and, with much thought and reflection, put my experience into some semblance of order and begun to write.

And as I sit here now, hand-writing my story, I realize why it took more than six years to begin. I now know that God did not allow me to start writing this story because He knew, in all of His infinite wisdom, that I needed to go through a healing process, and He definitely knew it would take a long, long time. I find myself shaking as I write down some of these details. I cannot really believe that it happened to me. That is one of the largest obstacles for me to come to terms with — that I did not recognize the true nature and scope of what was happening to me due to my own refusal and denial to believe and accept it. As it turns out, I was not at all steadfast in my own self-esteem. I was unable to stand up for myself because I had never had to defend myself, my emotional well-being, or my confidence in such a way. I was complete putty in his hands, and he would continue to mold and shape me into something I was unable to recognize.

For years I thought about writing a book but was unable to logically piece my experiences together in my brain. The truth is that most people in an abusive relationship do not want to believe what is happening to them. From the very first notion that abuse is actually occurring, most people — and that includes me — will immediately begin the denial process. Denial is good support, and one that you can hang a lot on, but I did not realize how negative and heavy denial becomes when you keep it around as a companion. I kept my denial so close that I was able to easily revisit painful experiences, re-opening, and re-infecting each wound again and again. Why do we do that to ourselves? Why do we stop on our life path, turn around, and go back to re-live the hurts we endured and left behind? It looks like some kind of self-torture, but really it is *doubt*. Doubt says, "it was not really that bad," and that "it would stop" and that "it had not really happened at all."

I have wasted so much time, energy, and tears going back up the path; doubting, denying. I have reached the point where I can refuse to continue to turn around. And as I begin this story, I vow to pick up the pace while pushing forward towards acknowledgment, acceptance, and truth.

The courage to face the story was critical, but so was the amount of healing. Taking these positive steps will be much harder to accomplish while trying to survive in my current environment. Prison is … well … Prison is many different things, none of which is very palatable to an intelligent, hard-working woman with morals, manners, values, and respect. Prison is, at best, a hard, evil, relentless pit of sadness and contempt that can lead directly to hell. However, I know now, at 54 years of age, that I am very capable of doing exactly what I put my mind to, now and in the future. Prison is full of evil, negativity, drama, drugs, and predatory women looking for someone to use, control, and abuse. I am always able to venture out of my quiet, safe room in search of someone who has it much worse than me. I do this on a daily basis and I never have to look very far. Sadness and insignificance are everywhere here, yet God allows me to rise above it with His favor and his grace poured upon my life. God has become one of the biggest blessings in my life. I have been able to completely lose my handy denial companion once and for all, and have replaced it with the much more positive, loving, and supportive company of acknowledgment, acceptance, and truth. Luckily for me, the loss of my denial companion meant that all of those issues that so easily hung from its arms are also gone forever.

# CHAPTER 2: GREAT BEGINNINGS

I had a wonderful upbringing in the most beautiful place imaginable, in the northern part of the lower peninsula of Michigan. Gorgeous rivers, bays, and lakes with each and every element of the four seasons playing out to perfection. Surrounded by Lake Michigan, tiny lakes and one specific river, the Boardman River, made for hours each summer season of swimming, tubing, and canoeing. The river was my absolute favorite place, and our little house on the hill in the Boardman Valley, where my mother still resides after more than 50 years, shaped and built me from the inside out.

The river was literally a few quick jumps down the hill, and we spent so much time there swimming, floating down on inner tubes and canoeing; always with friends or family members joining in. My mother would meet us at the door with a bar of soap and towels and send us to the river to bathe in our bathing suits before settling into our pajamas and going to bed. Sometimes she would direct us to the hose out in the yard to wash off the sticky, dirty events of our days spent outside playing and exploring in the woods and green hills — but we would beg to go to the river because it was so much more fun. She relented often, of course, with strict instructions to come right back.

My upbringing was awesome, and included large family gatherings, parties, weddings, and events full of fun, love, games, dancing, beer drinking, and eating. My parents worked extremely hard and we were not at all rich, but we always had everything we needed. They were outgoing and liked to have fun, always with us kids in tow. Dad and Mom loved us and supported us, communicated well with us while growing up and always let us express ourselves openly and honestly about anything. They were understanding and realistic about any punishment they handed down, and taught us to make our own mistakes, learn from them, and often said, "Don't ever call us if you need to be bailed out of jail" because, at that point, "if you are smart enough to get into trouble, you are more than smart enough to get out of it."

My mom and dad loved each other with passion and commitment and always stuck together through the good and the bad. The good times were particularly good, and the bad times not that bad at all. Their example in life and in marriage was extraordinary. I have known few people in my life who have stood up to that accomplishment. Marriage is hard work, and my experiences would be quite different than that of my parents — I failed colossally.

\* \*

For as far back as I can remember, I have always wanted to get married and have a family. I think this hopefulness was most likely due to the great experiences I had growing up with good role models like my parents. But my extremely high hopes for a long and prosperous future with each of my first two husbands came to an end, like so many others, over differences, problems, affairs, and general unhappiness.

I have had a deep love for men and deep lust for men. I have had dating relationships and, like most women, simply sexual relationships and one-night stands. I have had short-term relationships and long-term relationships. I have had close male friends and good working relationships with highly educated, professional, and well-established men such as lawyers, judges, and business owners. I have had three husbands.

My first husband is the father of my two beautiful children, but that union only lasted about five years. We were incredibly young when we met and married — both of us only 20. Marrying young is never a good idea because, as I now know, you lack so much experience and knowledge about so many things. But back then, he was handsome, outgoing, lots of fun and that was enough. We both had full-time jobs and made decent money, but really, we knew nothing at all about being a married couple. Having two little babies right away was awesome, and stressful. My husband was more interested in activities occurring outside of our relationship. In fact, he was never at home, always working late, hunting, fishing, or whatever else he could find to keep himself away. That made me the caregiver to the kids, doing all of the cooking, chores, running here and there and creating a stable environment for them while trying to maintain a stable mind. Thank God for youth, as that is the only thing that kept me afloat during those years of my life. Eventually, he began an affair and became involved in other nefarious activities, resulting in our divorce. Even so, we were able to put our differences aside and support a mostly healthy relationship through the years of the kids growing up. I was lucky to preserve a wonderful and loving relationship with his parents. They are awesome people and fabulous role models and grandparents to my kids, providing them with love, support, and companionship.

My second marriage occurred only a few years following this divorce and was very loving. It started with the typical scenario of a woman falling in love with her boss. Ron was a successful attorney partnered with one other man. The firm was small, but that was normal for a northern Michigan town, and business was good with lots of criminal cases, divorce and custody cases, collections, and general civil lawsuits. I mostly assisted his partner, Mike, as a secretary and became close friends with both he and his wife, Laila. Laila was the local Circuit Court Administrator and the four of us became good friends and spent time together double-dating, dining at gourmet restaurants, and gathering at each other's homes. These were some of the best times of my life.

Ron and I were both single, and we had lots of fun during our initial courtship with flirting and fun innuendo during business hours. He was incredibly supportive, and I grew to love him more and more. There was no jealousy or mistrust, and he always made me feel equal and on a level playing field. It was an incredibly good, ten-year relationship with mutual love, respect, and admiration. Ron really helped me believe in myself and made me feel beautiful. He spoiled me emotionally and monetarily, which I had not had in my first marriage. I believe that he really cherished me and appreciated our relationship. When I look back on it now, I realize that it did not end as abruptly as I thought at the time, rather, the relationship slowly deteriorated over a relatively long period. I remember feeling like I had been in love and part of an amazing marriage, then suddenly alone and divorced, as if it had happened overnight.

The truth is that I am to blame for that awful loss. I had become sick, mentally. I was severely depressed and unable to keep myself together. It began with the tragic loss of my aunt and uncle in a horrific car accident. To this day I cannot explain why this tragedy affected me to such an extreme, but it was a turning point in my life. I was also suffering severely from migraine headaches, a debilitating affliction that began when I was about sixteen. After being treated at a national headache clinic in lower Michigan on two separate three-week stays, my migraines were being managed the best they could be. But after the death of my aunt and uncle, the depression and headaches worsened, and I completely lost it. On more than one occasion I ended up in the psychiatric ward at the local hospital and was finally diagnosed with Bipolar Disorder and Chronic Depression. This was, unfortunately, the beginning of the end of my marriage. I was in and out of the hospital, taking many different types of psychotropic medications and narcotics, all pushing me into a complete tailspin. I began spending thousands of dollars on expensive jewelry to somehow fill the huge, unexplainable void in my life. That meant that I was incurring lots of debt, which I was hiding from my husband. Ron eventually filed for divorce, and, at the same time, began dating a newly hired female attorney in his office. It was over. I was alone again. And I blamed myself for all of it.

* *

It was a long, upward process for me over the next year or so. I held on tightly to my lessons of morals, manners, values, and respect. However, the belief and confidence in myself took many hits and, sadly, the result was a failed suicide attempt and more visits to the psychiatric ward.

Each time I entered the hospital I was able to collect myself and take many steps forward. I was always mindful of the many true blessings given to me by God. Blessings such as my family, friends, and children. The blessing to feel and love with my whole heart. The blessing to have a working brain enabling me to make a good career and a good living. The blessing to provide for myself and to survive and thrive daily in my life. So many blessings, most of which people take for granted and some of which are non-existent in other peoples' lives. Here, though, in prison there are so many women who have never been loved or cared for properly. Women who have never been afforded much of anything good and have no one on the outside waiting for them to come home. There are many evil women here, of course — murderers, child killers, child molesters, bank robbers, thieves, drug addicts — but there are also many good women who end up here because of bad decisions, something we have all experienced in our own lives. Nice, stable, good-hearted women who made bad decisions.

I believe that we all possess certain inner-tools, the most important and useful being our intuition — that gut feeling or that particular "tingly" sense that hits us like a warning siren, telling us to take notice, pay close attention, think it through again. For me, learning to listen to my intuition would take years. I eventually learned that not ignoring it, brushing it off, or dismissing it would be the most valuable lesson, the toughest lesson, ever. I know now that intuition is the voice of God's spirit within me and hearing it and acknowledging it will afford me many good things on my path forward.

If only I had listened closely to my gut feelings, my intuition, my spirit voice, I might never have experienced the wreckage, dismantling, and burial of my very self and soul.

# CHAPTER 3: MEETING HIM

I met my third husband while employed at the County District Court, serving as a clerk in the civil division — a transfer after three years in the criminal department. I was a "deputy clerk," which is not all that important, except it made me feel pretty cool when I was officially "deputized" by one of the sitting judges on my very first day. I loved my job with the Court and worked closely with other women in the front office. Our days were busy and full of excitement with community members and out-of-towners filing in and out, non-stop, to handle everything from simple traffic tickets, to paying fines, bonding someone out of jail, appearing for a Court hearing on a civil or criminal matter, or answering the call of a subpoena as a witness. It was a great opportunity to meet and interact with all kinds of people, professional and otherwise.

I had become extremely comfortable working for and around professional, well-educated people since I began my first position in a small law firm right out of high school in 1980. I stayed with that career path until I was arrested — a span of 28 years in total. I worked for many different attorneys who practiced in all areas of the law, and I would leave one job only to move to another which offered me more pay and benefits. While employed at the Courthouse it was a daily occurrence to work, talk, and become familiar with attorneys, judges, prosecutors, business owners, county employees, and police officers from the city, county, and state. I loved working in the law, and I loved dressing up and being professional.

This career path turned out to be a good fit. My upbringing stressed those all-important values of morals, manners, values, and respect, and here I was on the right side of the counter. I worked with the good guys — the guys who handed out judgements, fines and costs, jail sentences — in other words, justice. I loved my job and I was a happy, upstanding citizen. I had a lot of respect for upholding the law and, aside from one or two traffic citations, had never been in any trouble. Not one person in my large circle of family and friends had ever been arrested for a felony or spent time in prison — ever. I certainly never imagined — not in a million years — that I would ever be under arrest for anything. My life was running smoothly... However, I was unhappy in the relationship department.

Recently divorced for the second time, I was trying to get back on my feet emotionally and mentally. I still very much believed in love and was anxious and excited to begin a new chapter in my life — one that included love and, hopefully, happiness for the duration. I really thought that I deserved it. I was intimidated by the possibility of marrying for a third time — I had already been through it twice — and I surely knew what I did and did not want. What was frightening was the thought of being alone. I wanted to find "the one", the man who loved and cherished me as his wife, someone who wanted to be my husband and saw me as special. I had seen it growing up with my parents and I longed for it. I loved being loved by a man.

One day, in he walked. I was standing at the Courthouse counter, chatting with a corrections officer from the jail. The tall, handsome, well-built state police officer was very smiley, confident, friendly, and upbeat. He had the uniform, the hat, the gun belt, and all of the power and control such men possess in the position of a police officer. He carried it in his actions, and he carried it in his demeanor — his mere presence silently screamed power and control. He had a distinct swagger of arrogance, and at that first glance I decided he carried it well. He was, after all, the law — the one who protects and serves and makes the hard decisions and risks his life to save others. I thought his demeanor was deserved, as his position almost begged a touch of arrogance to be complete.

I think it was these first nuances that immediately cemented my trust in him and created an unwavering, unbreakable view of his character — he was exactly the man I wanted and needed him to be. This perception and what it meant in my own mind also cemented another feeling, one that would grow deep roots and intensify, slowly and methodically attaching itself to each and every element of my life over the next decade — that feeling was fear. The feeling of fear began as a soft whisper in my gut, one that initially I found almost erotic. After all, the fear felt natural with a man in his field and went along with his confidence, authority, power, and control. Over the coming years, it was a feeling that I would ignore, diminish, and dismiss time and time again. But in the beginning, the feeling of fear felt as natural as the emotion of trust which centered within me when I first laid eyes on him.

Fear and trust are a very unusual and oxymoronic combination, yet I was drawn in. After our first dinner date, we became a steady couple. We saw each other daily, and I now know that he led me into his life with a series of well-rehearsed qualities — his good looks, well-built body, his position. He was a true professional. He was an absolute master at his craft.

I eventually moved in with him after much persistence, persuasion, and promises that he would take care of me and pay my bills. I was 35 years old at that time, living in a rented apartment with my teenage daughter — with frequent visits from my son — and struggling to make ends meet. But I was doing it on my own and trying my hardest. I had even taken on a waitress job a couple of evenings a week in addition to my five days a week at the Courthouse.

I was exhausted, struggling with migraine headaches and managing different medications for both these and my depression. Despite the two divorces and all of my health issues, I was able to maintain an incredibly good relationship with my children, who both seemed happy and healthy. I have always had a deep connection and an honest, open relationship with both of my children. I let them speak their minds and discuss anything with me at any time. I was probably more of a friend to them than I should have been, but they were always comfortable coming to me with any problems or questions while they were growing up. I taught them the same important lessons that had been instilled in me — they knew right from wrong and never got into too much trouble.

After moving in with Paul (I do not think I have mentioned his name up to this point), he began talking about moving his career forward from being a state trooper to becoming a sergeant. He was in his early forties and had been applying for a couple of years but was denied each time. After living with him for about eight months, he got what he wanted. However, the new position came with a transfer to a different post, one that was four hours away from home. He immediately asked me to marry him and go with him. I was hesitant and unsure. I'd never lived anywhere else and I loved my hometown. My entire family lived there, as did all of my good friends. I was also very invested in my job at the courthouse and would be approaching ten years with the district court. I suspected that my kids would not want to leave their lives, which turned out to be true of my teenage son. My daughter, on the other hand, was torn. She was not at all excited about the prospect of moving in with her father and brother and going to a different high school.

Another reason I was unsure and hesitant was because of Paul himself. He could be odd and unusual at times, but the fact that my children and family members did not like him very much was extremely difficult for me. This was the first time I had ever gotten close to a man my entire family circle did not completely approve of, so it was really different. They were also concerned because of the problems I had experienced with severe depression the past couple of years. They thought he was controlling but agreed that it could be more of a protective thing, an attractive trait. I did feel very protected with him, and I was very much in love and excited about starting a new life.

Then, there was what I found out about Paul the first time we had sex. We were at my house, following a dinner date, and we ended up in the bedroom. I was very attracted to him and was excited to have a new sexual relationship. I am not a prude by any means, and sex is something I have always liked and enjoyed. Let's face it, we are all adults and we have all had normal, passionate sexual relations. Most of us have also had simply "fuck" sessions — pure, unapologetic sex with little to no emotions involved. I have definitely had those experiences and will be the first to admit how much fun they can be. My experiences with sex at that point in my life had been mostly passionate and loving, fulfilling but not unusual in any way. I had never had any desire to venture too far outside of the box. Rough sex or being tied up or any sadomasochist activities were never of any interest to me, and I had never been with anyone who had ever suggested such activities. I was comfortable with the sexual knowledge and experiences I had experimented with in my adult life.

So, you can imagine my surprise when I saw that his penis was pierced — not once, but twice. I was shocked beyond words and jumped off of the bed. I had never even heard of such a thing, let alone seen it. Back on the bed, my reaction was astonishment, with many questions. I wanted to know why his penis was pierced and, of course, when he had done it. I was also concerned about having intercourse with those piercings — one was literally hanging off the end of his penis, attached through the hole in the end and continuing through another hole on the underside of the head. It was about an inch long, with a metal ball on each end. The other one was made of thick metal, about one inch around in circumference and about 1/8th of an inch in girth. There was a metal ball holding the circle together. I had to take a good look at them, and my initial gut feeling was "this is really weird." He smiled at my apparent amazement and explained that he had done the piercing himself (yes, I just said that), as a "dare" when he was in college. This was back in the 1970s when no one in the normal world had ever heard of body piercing, let alone piercing the penis. I was very puzzled at first when he described it as a "Prince Albert" piercing, explaining that the big, round one was supposed to provide more pleasure for the woman, and the "bar" underneath was for his own pleasure. It really freaked me out at first until he told me he had never had any complaints or problems with any of his previous partners.

We ended up having sex that night, and the jewelry was really no big deal. I did question and wonder about it for months as I considered it odd for a professional, older man, but it became commonplace and normal. With his persuasion techniques played out to perfection, I soon decided that it was all okay, that he was different in an exciting way and his piercings were actually kind of cool. After all, sex was something I enjoyed. We never once used a condom, as I had my tubes tied after the birth of my second child and he reassured me he was disease free.

Wow, it is amazing how different this looks from the other side, the survival side — it feels really scary. While my family eventually supported my decision to get married and move away, I still had a huge decision to make. I did not choose wisely as it turns out, and my wrong choice would have a great impact on myself, my children, my entire family and so many more people.

But back then I thought everyone has some doubts, and as we began our life together, I was looking forward to the unknown. I was up for the challenge and provocation of seeing things from his point of view. We would be in this together, as husband and wife, two consenting adults — right? I trusted him and believed that he would protect me to the standard he had been trained to uphold as a necessity of his profession. I never could have imagined what was to come.

We were married on a cold Monday morning in November of 1999 at a very quick, nothing special ceremony at the Courthouse where I worked. We had both been married twice before and agreed that a third wedding party was not necessary. The magistrate was out of the office that day, so one of the judges I had worked for, Judge McCormick, conducted the ceremony. My parents served as witnesses. No one else knew that we were getting married. We were leaving on a trip to Oklahoma to visit his family later that day, driving twelve hours, so Paul suggested we do it as a surprise to everyone. He liked to visit his parents at least twice each year, and Thanksgiving was a time when his entire family would gather for the week. This was not our first trip to Oklahoma; we had already been there twice before and would make several more trips during our marriage, each one pleasant and eventful. I got along very well with his parents and each of his four siblings, and over the next ten years I grew to really love them. But it would become plainly evident to me that in his immediate family, my new husband was definitely the odd one out. The difference was clear and unmistakable, but one that would never be discussed at all, ever.

# CHAPTER 4: THE FIRST FEW YEARS

I remember the moving van parked outside our new house, ready to be emptied. I was really excited to be there, in a new relationship, setting up a new home. Paul did not have much of anything of his own. He, too, was recently divorced, and had apparently let his ex-wife have most of the material belongings. I really did not think twice about it since the van was full of anything and everything from my house, most of which my second husband had allowed me to keep when we divorced. So here I was, moving my entire life into Paul's house, and he suddenly grabs me by the hand, escorts me to the bedroom and proceeds to tell me that he had been having an affair with a married woman — has been for months. But, he said, he had made his final decision by choosing me and the affair was now over. He said he needed to tell me at that moment because he was feeling guilty. He had been trying to tell me but had been unable to say it. I was, as you can imagine, absolutely astonished and caught off-guard. Yet, somehow, he was able to convince me of his love and he made me feel important and special. He could be very loving and caring in those early days.

Yes, part of me was genuinely excited, but apprehension was the prominent feeling. Most of my apprehension was due to the fact that I was starting a brand-new life with a new husband in unfamiliar territory; far away from my usual comfort zone — four hours from the only home I had ever known, my children, my family and friends, and my beloved job. The trust and belief in his position as a police officer was first and foremost in my mind. Trust and belief along with a large dose of hoping for the best in our marriage and for our new life. We had discussed several times our mutual desire to stay married, to have a successful relationship, and we vowed to try our hardest to work on it together. I held on tightly to these things on a daily basis.

I tried to talk to him about his first marriage, but there was always great tension and not a lot of details. He did explain, though, that he and his first wife had been high school sweethearts, and that was followed by a 14-year marriage. Their entire relationship spanned over 20 years, during which they had two children. He admitted that it ended mostly because of his relationship with another woman, a woman he had attended the police academy with and fell hard for. He explained it as an "instant attraction." While he was being unfaithful with his "attraction," his wife became close to his best friend from college. The two of them eventually married and are still together today. But his real feelings were painfully evident by his comment on more than one occasion about his best friend that, "If he and I were to go into a dark alley, it would be a fight to the end and only one of us would walk out."

Paul did not have much of a relationship with his two older children who, oddly enough, I only met three different times during our decade-plus union. He told me that his relationship with them had been ruined by his ex-wife and his best friend. They had made it impossible for him to have visitation and turned the children against him by purposefully bad-mouthing him as their father. I believed that to be true — both of his older children seemed to despise him deeply and wanted almost nothing to do with him. I guessed that there were, most likely, many factors at play in the scenario, but he did not seem to be greatly bothered by it. I would, of course, learn much more about all of it later on in my journey — all of it terribly sad and, unfortunately, his own fault and his alone.

Something else that always gave me cause for wonderment was that Paul truly did not have any real friends, something he outright admitted to. The truth is that Paul was a very odd person. He was very smart — ingenious at times — but he had some very quirky traits; some things that were hard to figure out. He was extremely arrogant, which he never thought to apologize for, and which was, apparently, part of his makeup from a young age. He had no doubt that he was better and smarter than anyone else in the room, and he definitely knew everything about everything; annoyingly so. I simply accepted it as, "That's just Paul, that is the way he is," but it was much harder for other people to accept. Many people he encountered, or even worked with, disliked him, and considered him an asshole. This fact was hard for me because, unfortunately, every member of my family felt this way about him and simply tolerated him because he was my husband. People who knew and loved me were suspicious and skeptical. They believed he was too controlling. My father had many doubts about him and felt that Paul was disrespectful and disingenuous. My children grew to greatly dislike and distrust him because of his arrogance and know-it-all attitude, but mostly they were concerned about his control and manipulation. But they respected him as a police officer and were even fearful of him to some extent. There was just something about him that was off, something extremely hard to pinpoint. True enough, he was indeed an asshole at times, but I was in love with him and I was certain that he loved me.

I learned more about his second marriage shortly after we began dating due to the fact that he had a five-year-old daughter whom he adored. This second attempt at marriage was, according to him, disastrous, short-lived, and only really ever came to pass because of the child. His daughter spent a lot of time with him for visitation, and we travelled many miles across the state every other weekend to make that happen. His second wife, I think it is safe to say, hated him. Their daughter was born about nine months following their first date, but she refused to marry him until the child was three. They were divorced less than two years later. The two of them fought back and forth over custody, eventually deciding that the child would live with her mother during the school year, then spend the summer months with us. After several years on that schedule, his daughter lived with us most of the time. As a couple, we never went anywhere without her, including our anniversary dinners. We never had date nights and I often felt like the third-wheel with the two of them. It seems so strange to me now, looking back, and it is really hard to explain. She had no idea who he was as a man and was completely unaware of his oddities and unusual nature because she was a young child. She simply knew him as her daddy; the strong, important police officer. The last I saw her; she was only 15 years old and completely unaware of the situation unfolding in our house. I will most likely never see her again but will forever keep her close in my heart.

After settling into our rented house, which conveniently happened to be just a few short miles from Paul's new post, I was able to find a good job at a law firm in a well-to-do town. It was vastly different than what I was used to, but with my years of experience I was liked and appreciated at my new job. Not at all fortunate, however, was my hour-long-plus commute from home to work each way, every day, five days a week. I had banker's hours, so I was up early and not home again until after 6:30 p.m. most evenings. Since Paul was working different shifts every week, I had lots of time to myself.

Paul was making a decent income, and I was making nearly twice as much as I had at home. Initially, as expected, we had a joint bank account where all of our money landed. I had full access to the account with a debit card. I never had a credit card at all, which was perfectly fine with me because I felt I could buy what I needed or wanted without question. We could definitely afford it, I was certain, with our combined funds. We had an agreement from the beginning that he would be in charge of the finances and all of the tasks that came along with that chore since I really hated doing it — and I was really bad at it, as the past would indicate. Paul liked to be in control anyway, so there was never much discussion in this regard. I was definitely putting in my fair share as far as the bank account went, and I was comfortable going to lunch or stopping at the grocery store to pick up something we needed or something I wanted.

It became apparent, however, that all of this was definitely a trial period and that things would end up not quite how I had expected. In fact, over the next three years, every aspect of my life would change. For example, the time I had to myself turned out to be not mine at all. Paul was working the desk at the post, managing the troopers out on the road. Since we lived only a few miles from the post, he would request that I bring him dinner and sit with him, sometimes dining together while he worked. This became a pattern which quickly turned from a simple request to a demand. It was fine at first — he was all I had in this new place, he was my new husband, and we were beginning a new life together. But I quickly realized that he wanted me to be wherever he was almost all of the time. Some evenings I would stay with him for hours, practically begging him to let me go home. I was tired from working all day, I still had my good clothes and high heels on, and I wanted to relax, maybe do something around the house. I liked being alone and being by myself, something he did not. Some days, I would return home only to realize that he would be back soon himself, following his shift. I began to feel overwhelmed. That feeling was justified due to the fact that he was — I will say this as simply as I can —

very needy. He followed me around the house like a puppy, never allowing me to even be in the bathroom alone. He put one of our bar stools in the bathroom to sit on while I was in there — whether I was using the toilet, washing my face, or taking a shower. He also insisted that I sit in there while he was doing whatever he needed to do. He was not really mean in any way, at this point in time, and he never raised his voice, he just insisted. And I knew, somehow, not to question too much. In fact, I learned quickly not to question him at all about anything. That fear that I held in my gut, next to the trust, was growing.

He began expecting me to call him several times during the day, letting him know when I was leaving the office to begin my commute. I also needed to advise him in the morning when I left the house, and again when I arrived at the office. When I was not with him physically, I would never go more than two hours without talking to him on the phone. He knew where I was and what I was doing at all times. He was particularly good at never allowing me to be at home alone for any length of time, and I never once went anywhere after work or on a day off with anyone other than him — never. On the days he did not work, and I did, he began dictating the course my day would take to meet his expectations. When we both had the day off, he dictated exactly what we would do together. We never went anywhere socially, such as a movie, a play, or a sporting event. We ate our meals out most of the time, but we did not have any friends to share things with or invite over.

Soon he decided what I needed and did not need. I was not allowed to stop and buy anything on my way home from work, as he expected me home without delay. He took my debit card and cut it into pieces, even though my substantial income was deposited into our account. I only had cash in my wallet in the amount he thought to be sufficient, with no other means to pay for anything. After going back and forth with him about the debit card, he agreed to let me have another one when he realized that it was almost impossible to do everything for me. It did not take long for him to figure that out: We would do everything together, including the grocery shopping, putting gas in the car, and running simple errands. I was rarely out of his sight except when I was working or traveling there and back. He cut up the second debit card, then he removed my name completely from the bank account.

At one point he suggested that he begin driving me to and from work on the days he had off. I told him that was a ludicrous idea and pointed out that the trip would mean traveling at least four hours each day, back and forth — on his day off! — and for what reason exactly? I did not even begin to understand his thinking. He brushed off my complaints and chalked up his concerns to him wanting "to be protective." I told him in no uncertain terms that I was a big girl, a grown woman, and was very capable of getting myself back and forth to work. I did not really buy the "protective" argument he posed, but I really believed that he loved me. I was sure that he did really want to protect me.

I took this third marriage very seriously, and I was determined to make it work by doing anything necessary to accomplish that. Part of me was ashamed to be married for a third time, and I wanted to be a good wife to prove that I could be successful at it. I decided to dig deep, do my absolute best, work hard at making him happy — all the while clinging tightly to who he was as a police officer and hoping and praying it would all work out fine.

It was during this time that I began to diminish and dismiss what was happening as "it's not really that bad," "tomorrow will be different," or "it's not really what it seems." These thoughts made it much easier for me to live with and accept the reality. And honestly, I really believed it would not get any worse. What I did not realize then was that he was a master at his craft, and his plan was going very well. He was beginning to wreck me emotionally and mentally absolutely, comprehensively.

I am completely blessed and grateful that God was able to lead me — in this awful, negative place called prison — through the healing process. I am grateful for the pure strength, perseverance, and resilience He has instilled in my heart and soul to replace the wreckage and destruction that resided there for so long. My story, unfortunately, will get much worse and turn tragic, but I now believe that all of this has happened for a specific reason. I honestly believe this to be part of the process of me realizing God's exact purpose for my life.

# CHAPTER 5: ALL THINGS SEXUAL

I was aware from the onset of our relationship that sex was extremely important to Paul. After all, he was a man and all men crave and need sex in a different way than women. When we married and moved to Southern Michigan, sex became the usual topic at lunch or dinner — which was almost always in restaurants as we generally dined out. In a way, he seemed addicted to sex, and his increasingly odd needs and desires became exceedingly difficult for me to handle.

Slowly, deliberately, he began to be much more specific about certain things and would mention different or unusual activities to measure my reaction. He was very methodical in all of his actions, and his approach to sex was no different. It was almost as if he were writing a thesis or completing some sort of grand plan or blueprint in his brain, preparing to put it into action. My reactions differed depending on the suggestion and, initially, I was not exactly sure of his intentions. I did discover, however, that any positive or curious indication from me pleased and excited him, enabling him to open a door in a "green light" sort of way. What he explained to me was that, in his profession as a police officer, he was constantly having to be in control of every situation, and he tired of it. What he really liked, in fact, was to relinquish control in the sexual part of his life. In other words, he had discovered that he liked to be completely controlled in the bedroom and he made it clear that he wanted to be controlled by me. As his wife, I could meet his sexual needs and alleviate the stress and tension brought on by his profession. He presented this plan to me so positively, making me feel special for this way that I could make him feel better and more focused. It was like a precious, important gift that I, as his wife, could give him — one that could do so much for him. This gift was wrapped in love and the insistence that it was something he definitely needed, so much more than a mere craving. And he tied the gift up with the bright bow of his desire for me, his insatiable lust for my body, making his request attractive and alluring at the same time. I trusted him and believed he was giving me complete control over our sex life. I genuinely felt that this would bring us closer together, that it would allow us to express ourselves to one another in a positive way.

This notion of me being "in control" and "in charge" of our sexual activities diminished rather quickly. While his grand plan of softening me up, of testing the waters so he could run through that door he had so craftily opened became stronger. By the time I realized what was happening, I was playing the starring role in his deceitful, unwanted web of maniacal and twisted bondage and domination-filled fantasies.

From this point on, so many things changed in our relationship. And it is at this juncture in my story that I will attempt to describe and explain, to the best of my ability, how those changes occurred. I have the recollection of every event burned into my mind, my heart, my soul, which, unfortunately, makes describing the events the easier part. But the explanation of how I stepped through that door, how I lost myself and how I find myself here, writing in prison … that part escapes me. That part takes work.

He began taking me shopping to an adult-themed store where he purchased many items. While we shopped, he would repeat that these were things *I wanted to buy for him*, making it seem as though I were actually picking them out.

A dildo with a strap-on apparatus, a steel cock ring, a butt plug, a paddle, a whip, and a crop. Most of the time I was silent, but he would say things out loud like, "Oh yeah, this is perfect for you to use" or "This will work very well for you." He continued to try and make me believe that I was in control and using all of my own ideas and fantasies to please him, but this was a complete delusion. The truth was that I did not want or need any of those items. I was afraid of them being used on me. I was even more afraid of what he would request that I do with them on him. I was completely uncomfortable. I felt as though he was disrespecting my morals purposely. My thoughts and feelings meant nothing to him. His fantasies and needs became first and foremost, and I could keep my feelings to myself.

The entire issue of sex became scary. His thoughts regarding sex were like a scary monster. He soon gave himself the nickname of "slave boy" and he called me "mistress." I had a pair of thigh-high, black leather, stiletto boots and a black leather teddy he bought for me to wear as he tried his hardest to turn me into his personal dominatrix. He was into pain and demanded that I inflict it on him in every way imaginable. For example, during sex he would ask me to bite him so hard on his chest that it would bleed and turn black and blue. I would, at times, be in tears because of how much I knew it had to hurt. Mostly, though, it did not feel right to me and I hated it. I had never, ever hurt anyone on purpose.

Eventually he purchased a thick, black leather dog collar with a leash which he would wear whenever he was at home. He would sleep in the collar every night, sometimes with the leash attached and placed under my pillow. He became obsessed with my crotch and would suddenly accost me in the kitchen, the bathroom, or wherever I was in the house, pulling my pants down, performing oral sex, penetrating me with his fingers, or rubbing his erect penis up and down my butt crack. It was never done with kind words, a smile, or a suggestion of love or affection. It was always violent and maniacal. Sexual intercourse would always follow these attacks with no words spoken or love shown in any way. It was simply an animalistic sex act, and it occurred frequently.

After we had been married for about a year, he took me shopping because I was in dire need of new panties and bras. Of course, he would not let me go on my own — even at that early point I was not allowed to go anywhere alone. It also turned out that there was another reason for taking me shopping, a reason that became very clear as we browsed through the panties. He allowed me to pick out the ones I wanted, including the color and style. He then insisted that we get the exact pair in a larger size — for him to wear. He said he wanted to try women's underwear because he thought they would be more comfortable and not so hot, especially under his uniform. I was speechless at first, but again, followed his lead without questions. I was completely caught off-guard and sick to my stomach, but he became overly excited when he interpreted that I was open to the idea. We left Macy's that day with new bras for me and ten pair of exact, matching panties for each of us. Before we approached the counter to pay, I asked him what he was going to tell the clerk. Why so many panties, so alike, but in two different sizes? He responded that we would just tell the clerk that we were buying the extra ones for my sister. I was sure that my gut reaction and ill feelings were as obvious to everyone else as they were to me. But, of course, the clerk had no interest in questioning our purchase, which only proved how paranoid, doubtful, and skeptical I was becoming.

On the long, hour-plus ride home I tried to get some clear answers or an explanation about this new development in our sex life, but it was like pulling teeth. I made the obvious leap, in my opinion anyway, that he possibly had homosexual or transsexual feelings. He denied any such suggestion and became angry with me that I could think such a thing.

Each and every day following the purchase of panties, he would pick out which pair we would wear the next day, always matching them. He would make his decision at night, laying them all out on the bathroom counter so I would have no doubt. How many times in the following years would he check in with me during the day to make certain I was wearing the correct pair, either during a phone conversation or, if we were together, by looking down my pants? It seemed eerily important to him. But what really distressed me was the fact that he wore his civilian clothes to the post each day, then changed into his uniform in the locker room before his shift. I felt that my question was valid when I asked him exactly how he was going to explain to the other troopers — who might be changing their clothes to begin their shifts — why he was wearing women's underwear. At first, he explained that his locker was off in a corner, kind of out of the way, and he doubted anyone would notice. Then he said that if anyone ever asked him, he would just tell them, "My wife makes me wear them," which, of course, was absolutely ludicrous. I am sure that not one person who knew anything about him would ever believe that his wife would tell him to do anything, especially something so odd. That he would comply to such a request was even more laughable.

Not long after this shopping trip occurred, we went to a shop for some silk camisoles for him to wear. I was at a loss about exactly how to handle this very different behavior, and I worried more and more about the reasoning behind it. I was determined to get him to discuss it with me, so I again pushed the issue, this time approaching him more delicately and with more understanding. I let him know that I was there for him, that he could talk to me about all of his feelings and reasons for wearing women's undergarments, that I would not judge him. I tried to make him feel comfortable, assuring him that we could and would work through whatever it was together and figure it out. I explained that I just needed to know why, telling him it was a concern for me. In fact, many of the things he needed and wanted — demanded, actually — were real concerns of mine. However, he would not or could not come up with plausible explanations for anything. He would just get angry and tell me to accept it, period, because these were things he had to do. These were things he *needed* to do.

This was the pattern for our entire relationship about so many things — just accept it, he would say, do not ask questions because there was no explaining. I believe now, having had so much time to reflect, that he did not know the answer to this question or any of the other questions that arose over the years. How many times would I ask him to talk to me honestly, to open up to me about his obvious demons — all to no avail. Over and over again I would ask if he had ever been abused as a child — by a family member, an acquaintance, a stranger — only to incur his denial and anger. Although I was struggling to understand him, I was also more than willing to support him if he needed help professionally because I really did love him and care about him. Many times, during our marriage, I suggested that he seek help for his bizarre sexual issues, only for him to turn the conversation around on me and make me feel like a prude. Even worse, he would put me down by telling me that I was incapable of making him happy in the bedroom. I did not try hard enough to meet his sexual needs, he would say, and since he had so "unselfishly" given me this one and only task in our marriage, my complete failure was inexcusable and unacceptable. I really just wanted him to love me with passion and accept me and my feelings, but he was unwilling to do that. I have always enjoyed loving, passionate sex, but Paul did not seem capable of that.

My intuition was screaming inside of me. I became more fearful and unsure. I began to push back and resist him and his suggestions. But he did not care about or accept my resistance. And it was about to become much worse.

His overwhelming desire to "taste" me and "smell" me led to a new obsession. He began sleeping with my dirty underwear on his head, with the crotch area over his nose and mouth. He would take the panties out of the dirty clothes hamper and put them on his face, tucking them into his dog collar to keep them in place. I remember the first time I discovered this oddity. He would often be sleeping when I returned home from work because of his different shifts, and one night I went into the bedroom to let him know I was home. I turned the light on and saw my underwear on his head. I was shocked. I remember thinking, before I even opened my mouth to speak, "What the hell is going on here? This cannot be my life."

My questioning on this occasion led to the first instance of him becoming almost zombie-like in his facial expression. It did not last even a minute, but it would happen time and time again over the next six years whenever he seemed to not know or did not want to respond to my questions. He would be completely blank and stiff in his demeanor, with his eyes fogged over and his face twitching, almost as if his mind had shut down. It was so very odd and scary. I did not know what to think or what to do. I was unsure about questioning him under any circumstance, and I certainly knew to never say "no" to him. He did not accept the word "no" — period. I am not really sure how I exactly knew this, but I knew it well enough not to deny him or disagree with him. My intuition told me that this was best.

His expectations of me were becoming extreme. He had always criticized me for not shaving my legs enough, and he began insisting that I shave all of the hair from my body in every area. I had always kept a manicured crotch area before we met — I never liked a big bunch of hair between my legs, and it was natural for me to clean it up in the shower when I shaved my legs and underarms. Now, he insisted that my crotch be completely free of any hair, and I was expected to keep it that way. He began dictating exactly when I would accomplish this by determining what night of the week I would take a bath. He would sit on his stool next to the bathtub to watch me, and I would feel sick the entire time, each and every time, for the next nine years. He, too, would completely shave each and every hair from his body, which had always been the case from day one. It seemed so adolescent to me, but I could not bring myself to ponder that thought too long.

I found myself constantly walking on eggshells while trying to keep him happy. By this time, he decided everything, from where we ate to what we bought at the grocery store. I could not even make decisions about what was on the grocery list. If I started a list, he would cross off anything I wrote on it, or simply throw it away to start a new one — leaving my items off. What was this behavior? And why? I know now that it was a typical tool used by abusers — the need to control everything completely — but I did not recognize it for what it was back then. I was becoming more and more afraid of him, mostly due to the fact that I was not sure what he was capable of if he became angry. Even more importantly, I did not ever want to find out. He never showed too much anger, and only became violent in the sense of acting out in violence when he would hit objects or knock things off of the counter. This only happened a few times over the ten plus years we were together; however, when it did occur, it was truly frightening. He was not much of a yeller, and did not have a quick temper, but when his anger was released it would almost stop time. It would present itself like a roar of thunder or a bolt of lightning; quickly and with every bit of collected force. Explosive and real. Explosive and very, very scary.

My first encounter with his anger occurred in the kitchen one night when he was pouring a glass of milk. He poured too much, and the glass overflowed onto the counter, down the cupboard, and onto the floor. He became so enraged that he punched his fist into the top part of the refrigerator with such force that he left his knuckle-marks as a permanent dent. He seemed to be angry at himself, which I found to be very telling, especially in the years to come. When he became angry, and when what enraged him was his own fault, he became explosive and acted out with his fists. He would berate himself, calling himself names out loud and swearing. He would become completely pissed off and displeased with himself to the point of needing to become physically violent. He absolutely hated making mistakes and, while this did not happen very often, it had a huge impact on his mood for the rest of the day. This was a huge red flag to me, and every time it would occur my heart would sink to my feet and I would think, "If that had been my face that he planted his fist in, I would be dead."

To this point, however, I had not seen his anger directed at me or anyone else, and I was thankful. I would learn soon enough, though, that he only contained his anger to protect himself from any kind of backlash or irreparable consequences. Several times he said to me, "I am not stupid —— I would never hit you or leave a bruise on you because that would be the end of my career and evidence for you to use against me. I am smarter than that." To me, this statement made it very clear that he was certainly capable of bashing my face in. What was unclear was the assurance that he would be able to control his anger if I ever pushed him over the line — that fine, sensitive, breakable line.

That distinct line that he had completely and concisely drawn around our relationship made my fear real and almost constant. His ability to control and manipulate without needing to yell —barely raising his voice, and with so few words at that . . . it was completely uncanny. Yes, absolutely uncanny. Webster's Dictionary defines the word "uncanny" as: *mysterious or unfamiliar, especially in such a way to frighten or make uneasy; preternaturally strange; eerie;*

*weird; so remarkable; acute.* This definition could not be more perfect to describe him. It was the way he carried himself, the way he presented himself. His mere presence was in itself uncanny, and many people have testified to this fact. It was the very aura he emitted. You could definitely feel it, you could almost see it if you looked hard enough. It felt weird, bad, even evil at times.

Even so, I would often speak my mind, expressing my dislike or my discomfort with a certain act he demanded. My feelings and thoughts would quickly be dismissed and depreciated. He did not care what I thought or how I felt, disrespecting me completely. The more I tried to stick up for myself, the more he belittled me, making me feel bad about myself. The emotional and mental abuse took second place to the sexual abuse and the sexual weirdness, but I was crumbling.

# CHAPTER 6: DECLINING RAPIDLY

I was becoming depressed and my migraine headaches were beginning to overtake my life — the part he had not already taken over. I was missing days of work and I would be in bed in so much pain — vomiting, feeling completely drained emotionally and mentally. He hated it when I was sick in bed and his emotional abuse became much worse. He would pace in the bedroom like a caged animal, insisting I get up, take a shower, do something, anything but lie in bed. My inaction made him feel unattended and ignored, and that was a feeling he could not handle. He began to accuse me of faking my stress and my headaches, and insisted it was all in my head. He said I used those things as an excuse so I would not have to please him sexually.

I was now being abused sexually, mentally, and emotionally. His control and manipulation were devastating. I was running on autopilot and saw no way of changing it. He had not physically abused me in the sense of giving me a black eye or a large bruise —he never bloodied my nose — but the fear that he could and would hurt me in that way was foremost in my mind and I would shake inside even thinking about it.

Things between us were volatile, with my unwillingness to meet his sexual needs, my depression and headaches, and his belief that I was outright denying him. In his eyes, I was betraying and disrespecting him. Then, there was the fact that I missed home, my children, and all that I held dear in my heart, which also made him feel as though I was denying and disrespecting him. He wondered why *he* was not enough to make me happy. Why on earth wasn't I thrilled to be *his wife* and have the important job of *making him happy* by *fulfilling his needs and sexual desires*? In his mind, I did not need anything else. Time and time again he suggested that I take out my stress and discontent by physically hurting him in the bedroom. Beat him, bite him, make him bleed — whatever I wanted to do to him to make myself feel better. He thought that if I took all of my troubles out on him in the specific ways he demanded, we would both be happy.

This was not how I wanted to live my life. I did not want my life to be completely consumed with sex and all things sexual. Yet, he would have been thrilled if that had been the case. Every waking minute, for him, was about sex. All he wanted was to be at home with me doing nothing else but having sex, talking about sex, or being engaged in some type of sexual behavior. His entire life revolved around being at work, eating meals out with me, grocery shopping, mundane errands, and being at home — living, breathing, or performing sex in one way or another.

When he got his promotion and transfer, it was a given that we wanted to get back home to Northern Michigan as soon as possible. It had been this understanding that helped me decide to move away with him — I knew it would not be forever, I knew we would return home. True to his word, he immediately put his name on the transfer list, but the waiting time was normally about five years.

I wanted to go back home desperately, and he was very aware of this fact. But I also sensed that he was thrilled to have me to himself, hours and miles away from my hometown. I would say that he was threatened by my family and friends, and I know he was jealous of my children and the close relationship I had with both of them. After all, he did not have his older children in his life, and his youngest daughter, at that point, was still with her mother for much of the time. I think he needed someone he could treat as a possession; someone he could command and mold to fit his strange lifestyle.

This lifestyle, I discovered, was called sadomasochism. Webster defines sadism as *"the getting of sexual pleasure from dominating, mistreating or hurting one's partner; the getting of pleasure from inflicting physical or psychological pain on another or others."* And a masochist is defined as *"the getting of sexual pleasure from being dominated, mistreated or hurt physically or otherwise by one's partner; the getting of pleasure from suffering physical or psychological pain, inflicted by others or oneself."* Looking these words up in the dictionary absolutely astonished me — I always knew what they meant in a general sense, but their exact definitions are very telling now because they define him exactly, frighteningly so.

His oddity did not escape many people, and the uncomfortable feeling I encountered time and time again while being with other people in his presence was palpable. He was just plain weird in his mannerisms, his speech, his laugh, his actions, everything. I would be at the post, visiting him or delivering something he demanded I bring to him, even if it were just a Mountain Dew, and I could tell that even the troopers wondered about him. He made people feel uncomfortable with his uncanniness. I know there were many times that the other troopers would observe his behavior, see my reaction — which was usually me acting like a scared little puppy trying to make my master happy — and they had to wonder what was going on. My presence at the post became a daily occurrence. I had to bring a treat, his meals, and eat with him. Without a debit card or much cash in my wallet, I would have to stop at the post first, so he could either give me his debit card or enough cash to retrieve whatever it was he wanted. Then, I was stuck there until he was ready to excuse me. He would insist that I sit right beside him at the sergeant's desk, sometimes for hours at a time no matter what was happening. Calls would come in from a trooper looking for direction or wanting a person or a license plate run through the computer system, and I would just sit there while it all unfolded. I would try to excuse myself quietly by gathering my belongings, putting on my coat, and giving him a simple wave as I attempted to leave, but he would either grab me or gesture with his hand for me to sit back down. I was so embarrassed by his actions, and that scared little puppy feeling was painfully real.

After renting a house for two years, he decided he wanted to buy a piece of property about two miles from the post and put a modular-type home on it. I was completely against the idea for many reasons, the first being that I wanted to return home as soon as possible. Also, while the property was only a two- or three- minute drive from the State Police Post, it was at least twenty minutes farther away from where I worked. I was already spending at least four hours in the car every weekday to keep my job, plus we (mostly I) were driving back and forth on the weekends to get his daughter for visitation. Visits back home to see my children had been reduced to one weekend a month because of his schedule. Still, it was a lot of travelling, a lot of effort, and it created a lot of tension between us.

He bought the property, though, and then began searching throughout the entire state for a ranch-style, modular home. That took many weekend hours and late weeknights. Then, almost immediately after purchasing the property, our lease on the rented house was up.

So, there we were, homeless until our new house was completed. That's when he decided we would live at a motel until we were able to move. The motel he chose added a whole hour to my already long, hour-plus drive one way to work, but we stayed there for two months, with all of our belongings in storage and living out of a suitcase with no kitchen or microwave. It seems odd to mention this but living in a motel room with the bed in your face 24/7 made his sexual desires only increase. His activities were non-stop, and his demands became even more maniacal and strange. I began to regard them as sessions, and I will attempt to explain the elements of these sessions in detail, which will include some graphic details. There really is no other way because it is simply the truth. Please understand that the details in these activities may not seem offensive to some of you. However, when they occur with the intention of the purposeful infliction of pain — physically, mentally, and emotionally — with absolutely no sense of fun, love, or playfulness, that makes them much different. If he had asked for my input or considered my feelings, if he had initiated them with the slightest suggestion of flirtiness or posed them as a fun game, then that would have been an entirely different story.

Again, I am not a prude and have never been a prude. I have always been open to suggestions from my partner, with compromise and discussion. Sex can be really fun and enjoyable between two consenting adults, especially a married couple. But that was not the case with Paul. Sex was all he wanted and desired in his life. His sexual desires and his demons controlled him completely. We never went out or did "date" things like going to a movie, a social gathering, or a holiday party. Our life consisted of sleeping, eating, working, completing necessary daily tasks and being at home at a reasonable hour to begin the sexual activities he expected on a daily basis.

Activities in the sexual realm happened every day and could be something almost passive that he did to himself or a full-blown session that involved me. Minor things included things like him wearing his cock ring or butt plug all day, whether he was working or not. Or him sitting around the house while wearing only his dog collar and a camisole. Or maybe just being completely naked while wearing the collar and the leash. He also began tying his penis and testicles with a shoestring in a couple of different ways. He either split his testicles by running the shoestring between them and around each one to keep them completely separate. Then he would tie them so tightly that they would be completely without any blood flow and would turn dark purple, almost black. Other times he would gather them together and tie the shoestring around both of them, very tightly, with the same outcome. He would leave them tied up for hours, with sexual intercourse or masturbation finishing the event.

He was absolutely obsessed with masturbation, which always included me. He would lie on his back on the bed with me straddling his face, my crotch smothering his mouth and nose. He wanted me to smother him so that he was unable to breathe. This was an asphyxiation session he eventually needed to even have an orgasm. He never lost consciousness, though, because he would guide my movements by placing his hand on my butt. This particular session would sometimes go on for an hour or more. He confided in me that he often masturbated several times every day, even when he was at work.

I realize that men think about sex probably 100 times a day, or more, but this confession seemed very extreme. This sex thing, this sex "demon" he possessed, really possessed him entirely. I now believe (that hindsight 20/20 thing) that it consumed him to the point that he was unable to control it. In the end — and you will eventually agree with me — I believe he hated himself. His narcissism and arrogance, along with his position and stature, did not allow him to admit he was a sexual sadist — not even quietly to himself. I believe he fought with his feelings and emotions on a constant basis, but he was powerless to change. Maybe part of him did not want to change. On the other hand, he did have some good qualities which must have created incredible unrest in his soul.

During our long stay at the motel it would be a usual occurrence for me to beat his butt with the paddle or the crop or the whip, leaving red welts. He decided he needed a pair of handcuffs so that I could cuff his hands together or cuff him to the bed frame. Soon thereafter he brought home an "official" pair of hand and ankle cuffs that he had ordered directly from the police equipment catalog at work. He proudly put one handcuff key on my key ring with all of my other keys and left a second one in an envelope for me to store in my nightstand when we moved to our house. His next purchase was from Home Depot — several different lengths of chain, some steel clips that opened at each end and four thick, heavy eye-hooks which he eventually screwed into the head- and footboards of our king-size bed, one at each of the four corners. This way, I could cuff his hands and his ankles, attach a length of chain, then attach the four lengths of chain to each of the four eye-hooks. Face up or face down, he was completely unable to move. Even before the eye hooks were permanently attached to our bed, he would put these items to use time and time again while we resided in the motel room.

I was overwhelmed and exhausted — from all of the driving that I did each day, my eight-hour day at the law firm, the meals I provided from the hole-in-the-wall restaurant next to the motel, plus the motel room sexual sessions. I was becoming a complete wreck. I had been through a mental breakdown more than once, and I knew I was getting closer and closer to that point. I had learned to work through my headache days, realizing it was better to go to work than stay in bed to incur his disgust and abuse. To keep his verbal and emotional abuse at bay, I stopped doing certain things that I knew were effective to keep myself from falling into that deep hole of depression, like taking a long hot bath, baking a cake or cookies, or working on a craft project. There was no alone time, no "me" time.

Everything personal ceased with his absolute control over every waking hour of my life.

One of my favorite things to do to relax was to cook a nice dinner or bake a treat while enjoying a glass or two of wine. I had always been a social drinker with friends after work or during a night out, and would have wine in the house, with maybe a bottle of vodka or whiskey for when visitors showed up. Not only did Paul not drink a drop of alcohol his entire life, he had never attended high school parties or college bar nights with friends. There were never any "boys' night out" events for him. He never did any type of drugs or smoked marijuana, or even cigarettes. I did not do illicit drugs or smoke cigarettes either, but I had smoked marijuana in my teenage years. And I loved a glass of wine with dinner out or at home while relaxing. Since our marriage, all that ceased. He would not allow it. And it was not because of his religion. As a police officer he simply thought it was wrong and, in his eyes, it always led to some kind of trouble. There was no arguing with him. I tried bringing home a bottle of wine a couple of times, only to have him dump it out. I realized that it was easier to become a non-drinker in order to avoid his wrath. I, and most of my family, often wished he would drink a beer or down a shot simply to change his attitude, but it never happened.

His demands, his needs, and his abuse did not diminish during our stay at the motel and I began to get more and more migraine headaches. This caused a huge problem, as sometimes I would have to be in bed for two days at a time. With me in bed, there was no traveling, no meal deliveries, and I certainly was in no shape to be a sex slave. I made an appointment with a doctor who had been referred by a coworker. As I have mentioned, I had taken narcotics before, but not since moving away from my regular doctor. I had seen my old doctor for over ten years, and we had a trusting relationship. He had been through a lot with me.

There were times over the years when he would become concerned about the amount of prescriptions he was writing for me and we would work together to wean my use to a minimum.

When I went to see this new doctor, I really liked him. He had no problem prescribing narcotics with just a phone call to his office. This was great, as I began feeling much better very quickly and was able to function and get everything done. However, these prescribed medications were causing problems with Paul. He accompanied me to a couple of appointments and at first, he agreed that I functioned better with the pills, but he was concerned with how many I was using. On the other hand, he was happy with the change in my feelings and my attitude. I was not as unwilling or resistant to his sexual requests, mostly because I did not care much about it due to my highly medicated state. I truly barely remember much from this time in my life. I was basically numb with very few real feelings, which was a good thing because my emotions were, in a sense, given a long rest while turning me into a programmed robot. I worked and I made Paul happy by granting each of his daily demands. I do know that I was able to function well, get things done, and go, go, go. This would eventually come crashing down on me, but not for quite some time.

When we finally moved into our new house, I was running on fabricated fuel. My attitude and feelings began to swing wildly and reflected my bipolar diagnosis which, of course, was going to happen sooner or later. Paul became, I believe, almost bipolar himself with his inability to control me and my emotions. I would be in bed for days at a time with a migraine, coupled with over-medication, and he would pace back and forth in the bedroom and throughout the house like a caged animal, trying, somehow, to will me to "mental health" because he could not function without me showing him the attention he craved 24/7.

I would return to the doctor several times over the next months in an attempt to get myself under control. It was an ongoing trial-and-error period. Somehow, I was able to work and do everything that needed to be done, but it was up and down and back again, and our relationship was not weathering the storm well at all. Paul became very inward. He was never particularly good at showing emotion or being outwardly affectionate, but now he would go for hours without speaking to me. Days would go by when we would be like ships passing in the night, going through our daily motions, and not communicating at all. He had this ability to become a completely different person when he was unable to be in control. He would give me the silent treatment and pout like a child, hanging his head in disgust. I began denying him and standing my ground until he would make an effort to emerge from his shell and act like a loving husband. But the loving husband act would only last long enough to get me to comply with the status quo of being his sex slave. The sexual sessions would begin again, then my denial, then his cold war of silent treatment, pouting, and withdrawal. It was like a game of wills, and I actually enjoyed it. It was refreshing to go for days at a time simply existing together as roommates. I was able to breathe during these times of discontent. These cycles of my resistance and denial, followed by his withdrawal, followed by him becoming that loving husband to get his way occurred over and over again for the next year. During our times of coming back together I would try to discuss how I felt, asking if things could change with the sexual activities. We would agree to a truce: I would promise to do what he wanted, and he would agree to lighten things up a little. Inevitably, however, we would fall right back into things as usual. It was a vicious back and forth that was exhausting for me, and I'm certain he felt the same. Things became intense and volatile. He acted like a bomb ready to explode if I began any type of denial or showed any unwillingness to do what he wanted, so I caved in. It became apparent that keeping him happy and content was the best way to keep myself safe.

My children and parents began noticing a huge change in me during our visits north and they would ask me openly, out of his presence, what was wrong with me. I would explain it all away, blaming the drugs and my busy life. I would convince them that I was happy, but really, really tired. They accepted that, but held on to their concern because they knew, firsthand, that he was so controlling. My family also began commenting on my unusual absence from family dinners and extended family gatherings.

During my growing up and teenage years, my extended family stayed close through many different kinds of gatherings, like wedding showers, baby showers, weddings, picnics, dinner out on the weekends, etc. Now, the cousins I had grown up with and were close to were marrying and growing their families, so some kind of gathering or party was quite common on a regular basis — and I was missing in action. Paul would not allow me to attend these events. Even when a family event happened to occur on one of his days off, he would simply advise me that we were not attending. I loved these get togethers, and I missed spending time with my family.

My life was upside down and unfamiliar to me. I was becoming a person I did not recognize. Shortly after we moved into our new house and got settled, Paul began putting immense pressure on me to use the dildo with the strap-on part. He had been pressuring me since he purchased it, but somehow, I had been able to shut him down. But, as I mentioned before, I was having trouble experiencing any real feelings about anything at all due to my narcotic use and, after days and weeks of begging and manipulation, I granted his wish. By this time all of the hooks had been screwed into the four corners of our bed, so the mere thought of me chaining him to the bed and using the dildo on him became an absolute quest and desire. For me, it was awful and demeaning and made me nauseous. He knew I hated it, and I was certainly not able to accomplish it exactly to his standards, but it became a common "session" activity. He also demanded that I simulate oral sex with that same dildo, something that made him extremely excited. Yuck, I thought — was he really gay? Did he desire men? Was he bisexual? I had no doubt he desired women and what they could provide him, but that did not seem to quench his insatiable, never-ending desire for alternative sexual pleasure.

I told him I was beginning to wonder if I could ever do enough to satisfy him and shared my concern — and assurance — that he would eventually need to go outside of our marriage to have his increasing needs and desires met. In the coming years, I would bring this up time and again, only to have him deny the thought and insist that he would never do such a thing. I was not convinced then and would not be at any time in the future.

About this time, he also began insisting that he "clean me up" following sex by licking and sucking his sperm out of me. He would begin this by asking me during intercourse if he could clean me up immediately following, and when I would agree he would become more and more excited at the thought. I hated this, too. I thought it was absolutely disgusting. But if I showed any sign of refusal — by saying nothing or that I did not want him to do that and attempting to quickly get away to the bathroom — he would pull me back onto the bed and get his way.

As disgusting and degrading as I thought that was, what he suggested next was the single most degrading and demeaning act in his arsenal of sick fantasies. It would occur each and every day for the next several years, and eventually become the one act, the one daily event, which would cause the most damage to my being. There would be more, possibly worse acts of abuse that would follow and continue until the end of our lives together, but this particular act of extreme, intentional infliction of mental and emotional abuse and anguish remains the most completely devastating. This act involved his obsession with my urination. Back when he was "testing the waters," he brought up the subject of a "golden shower." I had heard of or read about this at some time in my life — it is where you or your partner urinate on each other during sexual activity. I guess that is what it means. I had never really given it much thought, due to the fact that I was positive I would never consider engaging in such a thing. It was completely against anything and everything I was ever taught or believed to be right in my life and I had absolutely no interest in experiencing it. His idea of a golden shower was much eviler and more outlandish, in my opinion, than anything I had ever read about. He wanted to come into the bathroom with me, have me sit on the toilet after completely undressing from the waist down, and then, while he lay on his back on the floor in front of me with his head at my feet, face up, mouth wide open, have me squat down and urinate into his mouth. He would swallow all of it and then he would lick me clean. I was not allowed to use any tissue to wipe myself. Finally, he would watch me get dressed and leave the bathroom. I wanted nothing to do with it. I was sickened, turned off, and appalled at his suggestion and told him that it would never happen. Of course, he became angry and disappointed at my outright refusal. We were once again at war.

* *

During the rest of the time we lived in lower Michigan, I submitted to each and every one of his demands except this one. I continued my staunch stand of repudiation. But he hounded and stalked me. He did not care about my feelings or requests. He especially did not care about what these things were doing to me emotionally and mentally.

Physically, I was having problems, too. His piercings were causing numerous bladder and bacterial infections.

It seemed to me that he had become completely incapable of being happy or content. He never laughed out loud anymore, and rarely even smiled. He was only interested in one thing — the one thing that he said made him happy — and that was sex or anything sexual in nature. But I had seen him be talkative, jovial, and somewhat pleasant at work or while spending time with his daughter and I started to believe that he possibly had more than one personality. I started to believe that he had me in his life for two purposes only. For one, I was a good "front" for him. When he needed to appear normal and grounded, I was the good wife. The other reason was that it was easy for him to use me, control me, dominate me, intimidate me, shame me, guilt me, belittle me, isolate me, manipulate me, diminish me, disrespect me, degrade me, stalk me, scar and bruise me as a person, and make me live in fear. This is what seemed to make him happy. This is what boosted his self-esteem and confidence.

After months of arguing about the "urination issue," it came to an end one day when I locked myself in the bathroom. He beat and pounded on the door, eventually searching for and using a key to enter the bathroom in anger and unrelenting insistence. I gave in. I believed it was better to accept something that I knew about rather than something I did not know about — his wrath. I did what he wanted, and it took every ounce of energy and determination. When he exited the bathroom, I sat there on the toilet feeling wrecked, worthless, and dirty. It was not hard to feel this way. These specific feelings had been sitting at the top of a long list of bad feelings, feelings which had been building and building in my heart and soul, all courtesy of his intentional actions and abuse. I sat there on that toilet unable to move or think straight for an awfully long time, the tears flowing down my face. I wished I could somehow drown or choke on them. Later, I cried for hours in our room. I remember this as being one of the few times in our entire marriage when he actually left me alone to live in the misery he had caused. Maybe it was easier for him to distance himself, so as to not incur any guilt or shame at what he had caused. I went to sleep that afternoon, and when he came into the bedroom around dinner time to wake me up and suggest we go out to dinner, it was as if nothing at all had happened. Everything was going on in its normal, predictable fashion. He did not suggest the urination thing again for a short while. Eventually, though, after much consternation back and forth, it became a daily occurrence with no discussion whatsoever. It was expected, period.

This one act of abuse would take more from me emotionally and mentally than any other act thus far or yet to come. The deep feelings of worthlessness and insignificance would overtake me each and every time that I was forced to endure this abuse. It would continue to build up and strengthen for years, hardening into complete hatred, contempt, and disdain.

It was at this point in time, three years into our marriage, that I began to seriously think about leaving him. Just as fast as that thought came, though, I knew that I was not capable of it, for many reasons. One reason was my mental health — I just could not trust myself. Another reason was isolation — I did not think I could leave him on my own. I was too far away from home. I was stuck, and all I could do was hope and pray that we would be transferred home sooner rather than later. My prayers were answered almost immediately. He got the call for us to return north, maintaining his sergeant's position. I was thrilled. Soon I would be surrounded by my children, my family, and my friends. I was sure that I would be able to breathe more freely and get some counsel regarding the course of my life. Even though I had the inclination of ending the marriage,

I was hopeful that the change of scenery would improve something, anything, in my relationship with my husband.

There were some especially important things that needed to occur first, the most important being selling the house we had lived in for less than a year. I was certain this task alone would hold up the process for longer than I wanted, and I would do whatever was necessary to make it quick and smooth. As it turned out, Paul's transfer included orders to begin his new job at his former post within two weeks. He put the house up for sale immediately, and then he was gone. It took approximately three months to sell the house, and during that time many things occurred, most of them to my detriment.

With Paul gone, I was left to continue working and stay put until the house sold. Yes, I did have some time to myself during these three months, but it was not at all relaxing or soothing. Each and every weekend I was expected to travel north to see him — a round trip of over 400 miles — while also trying to visit with my children and family. Then, twice a month there were the visits to see his daughter, adding many more miles, completely in the wrong direction. I was exhausted and diminished from his demands and abuse, and with my migraine headaches and the ongoing narcotic use I was cracking up, breaking apart. My already intense life was becoming extreme. But every once in a while, I would hear a voice, loud and clear, telling me to "get help – and get it soon."

It is extremely hard for me to read this statement in my own handwriting. Admitting it to myself is even harder. I was never the person who habitually thought things were too hard or too overwhelming. I had always been able to overcome feelings of being tired and overwhelmed because I had always had some control over making myself feel better, even if that meant admitting that I needed professional help. My family members had, at times, made that final decision for me, with my agreement, but they did it out of love and concern for my well-being. It is not easy living with severe depression or feeling mentally and emotionally fragile, particularly if there does not seem to be a reason for it. It is a very desperate feeling, and I thank God that I was never ashamed to admit that I needed help. I thank God that my family was always there to help me when that was necessary, to insist on that help out of love.

# CHAPTER 7: BUILDING AND TEARING DOWN

Paul was living in a motel room in Traverse City that had been provided by the State Police Department, a benefit of the transfer to a new post. It was dark, old, and very depressing, and I moved in with him; we rarely had any visitors. My children and family all agreed that it was like a dungeon and no place to hang out. Paul had decided — completely ignoring my input — that he wanted to build a brand-new house. He refused to even consider renting for a year or so until we settled and figured out which area suited us best. While he looked for some property and a builder, he also decided to move us into a different motel. We were basically living out of suitcases again, but at least this one had a kitchenette. Still, I was feeling really anxious because his ten-year-old daughter was going to be staying with us for the summer. The motel room itself was not at all conducive for a long stay with a ten-year-old — it was simply one big room with two queen-sized beds, a television, a small kitchenette, one chair, and a separate bathroom. We would basically be living on top of each other with no privacy whatsoever. The sexual activities had not changed or reduced. I was concerned about her being there with us.

It was almost spring, 2003, and I really wanted us to buy or build close to town, where the post was, where my job was — very quickly, I had gotten a job at a fairly large law firm where I knew some of the attorneys and support staff personally. I really thought he would prefer to live close to the post too, as that was always his biggest concern when we lived down-state. But he insisted on looking outside of the county. He found a five-acre piece of property near a small town that was really just a blur, not to mention a 30- to 40-minute drive to work, shopping, restaurants. No matter. He was running the entire show and I was too tired and too wrecked to really care. He went ahead and hired a local builder to build a nice two-story, three-bedroom house — a long process. We ended up living in that motel room for eight long months.

Paul increasingly secluded and controlled me while waiting for the house to be built. Any indications that I wanted to visit my parents, go out to a meal with my children, or go shopping were immediately frowned upon and replaced with an activity that he needed me to do. The motel was a short distance from my office and his post, and it became an everyday occurrence for me to provide him with lunch or dinner, some days both, depending on his shift. If I left my office on my lunch hour at noon, for example, I could pick up his food, deliver it to him, then be back to my office by 1:00 p.m. Like before, some days I would have to stop at the post first to get the cash to buy what he demanded, only to return as quickly as possible to deliver it to him and get back to my own job on time. If he were working later in the evening, I would be required to go through the same process immediately upon my leaving the office at 5:00 p.m. to provide him with dinner. We would then eat together at his desk and I would leave only when he allowed me to go, usually about 7:00 or 8:00 at night.

These actions alone made it impossible for me to have lunch or dinner with any of my friends or family. Then, there was the money. He would usually place a twenty dollar bill in the wallet inside of my purse at the beginning of each week. If I spent it by Wednesday, buying food for him, he would give me more cash, but only if I returned all of the change after retrieving his meal. He was constantly checking my wallet and every corner and pocket of my purse, questioning me immediately to explain why I had little or no money left. Remember, my name was not on our bank account, and my paychecks were immediately deposited into his bank account on the same day I received them, either by me with a deposit slip he had provided to accomplish the task or by him — he regularly showed up at my place of employment, but only to get my money from me. Over the next few years, he would even show up on the days I was absent, insisting that they hand over my paycheck.

Months and weeks went by. We were still in the motel and I was getting more migraine headaches, more depressed. I had reconnected with my old doctor, and he was not happy at all that I had been prescribed narcotics again. He refused to give me any at all, "simply for my own good," he said. I thank God for his decision now, because continuing on that path of narcotics very well could have killed me. Both of my children and several of my family members had clearly noted my apparent stress and the obvious change in my attitude and demeanor. Of course, I had never hinted to my family, or anyone, what I was actually experiencing, and because of Paul's position with the police force, they were not comfortable butting in or making assumptions. In fact, they were somewhat fearful of him. My silence and their trust in his position made them respectfully keep their distance.

While I was excited to finally be home, I soon realized that, as usual, nothing would be as I had imagined. His control, manipulation, and abuse in this familiar setting worsened. I can look back now and see it clearly, but at the time I was completely blind and, unfortunately, very naive. Blind and naive are both very appropriate ways for me to describe my feelings. In fact, he felt threatened to have my children and family so close. As such, he would have to erect some much tighter parameters around me and keep my activities under strict control in order to avoid any questions from them. This house, so far away from everyone, was part of his plan. Keeping me secluded made everything easier for him. It was a good plan and it had worked before. When he married me and moved us away, he was able to bend and shape me. Those three years had done their damage and I was his puppet. He had changed and molded me into this fragile, meek, and silent woman. A woman who would not speak up, completely inward and fearful.

How did this happen to me? Where had my strength and my confidence and my voice to stick up for myself gone? I felt stupid and inferior to my real, true self, and I could not understand how that had happened. Yes, I really did feel stupid. I really felt that, somehow, I had "let" this happen to me.

* *

Returning home was a complete failure and I was unable to make any of my own decisions about my life. I felt stuck and unable to move. I felt like I had become a completely different person, someone I did not recognize at all. Even more devastating, I was someone I did not like at all.

Everyone saw it; the huge change in me. I finally saw it for what it was exactly, and I blamed only one person for it. Him — Paul. Paul made sure that I was unable to do anything other than be at his beck and call. I was his everything. Slowly, methodically, intentionally, he was making me into his slave — a slave that would do anything and everything he demanded. I began missing more and more work, and in my twenty-plus years of successful employment, I was fired for the very first time. It was absolutely devastating, but honestly, I felt wrecked and incapable. With all of these things compounding at the same time — the control, manipulation, and abuse by my own husband; the inability to spend quality time with my loved ones; the loss of my job; and the fact that his young daughter was about to join us for the entire summer in the motel room — it was all too much for me to handle. I lost my will to live.

It was a Monday night, Memorial Day night in 2003, that I decided to attempt suicide for the second time. I felt utterly lost and completely alone. I was as cold and hard as ice inside. That felt horrible and I had no will to move forward in this current life, a life that was different and unrecognizable in every way. Like the first time I attempted to kill myself, I was at the end of my rope.

He had gone to work at 2:00 p.m. that afternoon, and I was at the tiny table in that awful, dark, depressing motel room. I wrote a note to my loved ones telling them I was just too tired and depressed to continue living. I also made a short statement about Paul being too controlling and that I did not want to be married to him anymore. I remember explicitly writing how I longed to see Jesus' face and wanted to rest in his loving arms. I then proceeded to take every pill I could find in that room, all of his prescriptions and mine, several hundred pills in total. Then I lay down, crying and praying, feeling completely helpless.

The next thing I remember is him carrying me into the emergency room. I had survived. Rather, I was saved by the person from whom I was trying to escape. After three days in intensive care, they admitted me to the psychiatric ward and, for more than two weeks, he visited me every day. He seemed truly shaken at my suicide attempt and cried while repeatedly apologizing for his controlling behavior. He promised that the sexual abuse would cease. That note I had left on that tiny table in our motel room, however, was never discussed, never mentioned by either of us. Somehow, it had managed to disappear, never to be seen by anyone other than Paul himself. He pretended that it never existed, I never brought it up. Remember, I had not spoken a word to anyone about the abuse I was suffering, and even at this low point it felt impossible to admit it to my own heart and soul. Paul never asked me the obvious question of why I would attempt to take my own life, either. I have always believed in my heart that the reason is that he knew the answer all too well — and he definitely did not want to hear me say it or discuss it in any way.

There was more disappointment when my doctor refused to let me attend my son's graduation party. Chad's father and I spent months planning, and it was to include a large crowd of family members from both sides, food, drinks — a celebratory day for our son. The party was held just a few days before my scheduled release from the hospital, and missing out only deepened my depression and gave Paul yet another golden opportunity to talk about my failing mental health and how he was just trying to take care of me like a loving, caring, strong husband. No one questioned him.

What I did not realize — and would not learn about for years to come — was that he had begun telling everyone he worked with — and anyone else who would listen — that I was really "sick" and mostly unable to care for myself. Several troopers apparently asked him why he stayed with me, all of them suggesting he divorce and move on with his life. They could not understand how he was able to put up with all of my problems. But he presented himself as the patient, loving, savior husband. He would puff up his chest and brag about how he was taking such good care of me, how much he loved me and how he would never think of leaving me. He shed tears at church and asked people to pray for me and for our marriage to weather the storm. He used my fragile state to gain sympathy and support for himself and his iron-clad ego. This classic "poor me" defense became the perfect ruse for keeping the attention away from the bitter truth — that he was an abusive, sick, and evil man.

This ruse was used on everyone in my entire family, and he would tell his parents and his siblings the same story. I admit that it was very believable, what with my past mental history and attempts to commit suicide. My family certainly saw the change in me, but as they had no idea who he really was, as a husband or a man, his "patient, loving, savior husband" speeches only elevated him in their minds. They still did not like him much, but they continued to believe him and trust that he was doing what was best for me. Yes, things were pretty perfect in his life. He had me right where he wanted.

Which was back in that motel room. The sexual abuse did come to a halt, to a certain extent anyway, because his daughter was there for the three-month summer visitation. But the status quo continued everywhere else, with me running back and forth to the post with meals, snacks, and drinks at his request, all with his daughter in tow. The sexual activities were reduced to simple, quiet intercourse after she had fallen asleep late at night. His antics of accompanying me in the bathroom also continued as usual, and the urination thing went on without any interruption at all. But it became a more settled time for me, those three months, because so many of the sexual demands and expectations were absent. That time felt like a reprieve because of the change in his demeanor and the lessening of his demands.

His daughter left in August to begin school and I found a different job at another law firm. We finally moved into our new house in October of 2003 and got settled in. But from this point forward, my life is a blur. Over the next six years, I would work at a job for several months only to quit and stay unemployed for several months. The headaches and depression, the fact that I did not and could not recognize myself anymore kept me isolated and in bed. I did not like who I had become, and he desperately hated it when I was sick and in bed. He began using these occasions to degrade me, belittle me, and make me feel worthless and incapable as a person — and especially as a wife.

Then, he suddenly became interested in going to church. He knew this would be incredibly significant to me since I had grown up going to church with my mother, always believing and relying on God as my savior. Paul and I had never discussed religion or attending church regularly, so his sudden decision to join both of my parents at their church made me very happy. We began attending every Sunday. It was a welcome, uplifting change and provided me with added strength. Paul had always played the guitar, and he began playing in church with the praise and worship team. I was hoping and praying that this would be the change that our marriage desperately needed.

I believe in my heart that he was looking for some solace and an escape from his own demons which were out of his control. And I know for a fact that God was working in his heart, but He was unable to change Paul's sexual desires. Paul was so put-out and angry at my continued depression and inability to meet his sexual demands that he simply began taking what he wanted. He forced himself on me and raped me. He was very assertive and violent, with no emotion or words spoken at all. He would force himself on me almost every morning before he left for work, and often at night when he returned home from a late shift. After my suicide attempt, he had stuck to his promises of stopping all of the unusual sexual activities — but that only lasted a short time. One by one, all of the old ways were reintroduced into our new bedroom, without discussion and with more intention and insistence than ever before.

The urination issue was by then a daily occurrence, and to get his sadistic fix he even began accompanying me into the bathroom at my parents' house. I look back at that and realize what a sick slap in the face that was, not only to me but to my mother and father as well. They would often ask why we had to be in the bathroom together, never knowing the exact reason. My own children would question this same action time and time again, and after several years, my response finally settled on, "You don't want to know." They stopped asking.

Our new house became an extremely uncomfortable place. Fear was a common and palpable feeling in the air. My children realized quickly that keeping Paul happy by not making any waves or causing any problems was the best for all of us. During the six years that we resided in that house, my own parents only visited three or four times, and my own siblings only once or twice. We never had family or friends over for any occasion. It was easier for everyone to stay away and stay out of it.

Why couldn't I tell anyone about the abuse? Well, mostly because of the shame and disbelief it caused for me. But also because of Paul's position as a police officer and the "band of brothers'" scenario within every police force everywhere. Who was I supposed to call for help? He always reminded me that no one would ever believe me anyway, because he was so important, and I was mentally sick. I was a meek and mild woman attempting to ruin his illustrious career for no reason. In my mind, I could not call the police on my own husband. He was the police.

# CHAPTER 8: H.M.F.I.C.

Paul was a tall, strong man, about 240 pounds, 6'2", with strong muscles in his entire body. I was only 5'5" and weighed anywhere from 130 to 140, depending on my stress level and eating habits. His hands were particularly strong, and they were so wide from side to side that he was unable to put his little finger to his thumb. He was good at making me fear him.

I never knew what mood he would be in when he came home from work, but I could easily tell when he was not happy. He would slam the door when he came home and throw all of his things across the kitchen counter, knocking everything else onto the floor. Some days he would come home and complain about why the washer was running or why there were clothes in the dryer. He would question me as to why I was running the water in the kitchen for so long or why I was going out to the garage or looking in the closet upstairs. Who was I speaking with on the phone and why? Many times, he had come home to find that I had prepared dinner, only to show his disappointment at what I had cooked or declare that he had made plans to eat out instead. He questioned each and every move I made. I could do absolutely nothing to his standards.

Eventually, he took away all of the domestic chores that a normal wife handles, such as the cooking, which I had always loved to do. The grocery shopping became a once-a-week task, and we would drive to the Meijer store with the list he had made himself. I was required to walk at his side or right behind him while he pushed the cart and did the shopping. I learned quickly not to venture away from him because he would search for me immediately and remind me I was not supposed to leave. I also learned that I was not allowed to put anything in the cart that I wanted or thought we needed. He would look at me like I was a 12-year-old child and instruct me to "go put that back." At times he would gesture his expectations with his hands, commanding me without speaking. I remember saying to him a few times, "I do not respond to hand commands, I am not a dog," only to do what he insisted anyway.

Of course, we would often see people I knew while we were shopping, but if I stopped to have a conversation, he would grab my arm to keep me moving. Those were truly awkward situations. The friend or acquaintance would stare at me with a question mark written on their face and I would just look at them helplessly. He was never friendly to anyone who tried to speak to me. My world became smaller and more secluded. He was the man in charge, and I was the inverted child following behind him wherever we went. He often referred to himself at work and at home as the H.M.F.I.C. — "head mother fucker in charge."

When we moved into our new house, he initially put a television in our bedroom, only to take it out and move it to the basement because he did not like the fact that I would actually watch it in bed. He felt very threatened and left out when my attention was turned on anything other than himself. If I were watching television in the living room when he came home from work, he would walk over, grab the remote, and turn the TV off without saying a word. He did not have to speak as his actions spoke volumes. He also made it very clear, without using words, when it was time for bed. He would suddenly turn off all the lights, the television — no matter if I was watching or not — go to the bedroom and pull all of the covers off to the end of the bed. That was my cue that it was time for me to get busy pleasing him. No questions, no arguing, no communication whatsoever. I once had a partner who would suggest it was time for bed with a nice, "Hey, ready for bed?" or "How long before you'll be ready to take it in for the night?" or simply, "Let's go to bed." Isn't that how it is for most people?

He was never kind or considerate. I thought it was rather cruel that he never once, in our ten-plus years of being together, said "Excuse you" or God bless you" when I sneezed. He would respond in kind to anyone else who sneezed, but never to me. He never, ever told me that I looked nice or that he liked what I was wearing. I was a professional woman who worked in law offices, and I always dressed up and did my hair and makeup every day. I think he preferred that I look not attractive. He scoffed at my leather coats and my nice shoes and said that I liked to wear them because they brought me attention. I made many changes to make him happy and quiet his constant criticism. I had a lot of really nice clothes, too, from my second marriage. Paul refused to let me buy anything new to wear, even if I needed it. He would point out that I had a closet full of nice clothes and shoes and insist I did not need any more.

He was also turning into a paranoid husband figure. He would often see tire tracks in our driveway and insisted that someone had been at the house while he was gone. He accused me of hiding things. He would call me several times a day to check on me and determine my whereabouts or ask what I was doing. If I did not answer the phone the first time — because I was in the shower or the laundry room — he would hang up and call right back. In the last few years we lived in that house; he would often send a trooper to check on me. Sometimes the trooper would just be driving by, sometimes he would come up the driveway to see if my car was there. It was crazy behavior and very concerning to me.

Shortly after he removed the television from our bedroom, he replaced it with a brand-new computer and large monitor hooked up to the internet. He was a very smart person when it came to computers and all things technical, so the computer in our bedroom was a welcome addition (for me) which took up a lot of his idle time. When he first brought it home and was setting it up, I went in to see how things were going. I mentioned that I would like to sit there for a short time with him so I could set up an e-mail account. He advised me that he had already done that and pointed to a piece of paper on the desk which had my username and my password written on it, both of which he had chosen for me. He said that I should not even think about changing it, because he had disabled that part of the program. He made it clear that I was all set up, but that he would be checking my account on a daily basis to see my activities and who I was communicating with. I threw up my hands in disbelief and told him not to bother because I would not be using it at all. He was, of course, happy with my decision and gloated at his ability to keep me in check.

I never did use that damn computer, except to revamp my resumé and make some cover letters when applying for a job. He, on the other hand, was glued to it, searching for all things sexual. I knew, obviously, what he was up to. I was aware that he was visiting porn sites and looking at very evil things, only because he would call me into the bedroom and show me an image simply to get my reaction. My reaction never changed from disgust and disbelief, but it is my true belief that he was always hoping for something positive or inviting from me. How could I react in any way other than pure horror? The images that excited him always contained a woman, or some part of a woman, crying, bleeding, looking terrified, chained down or tied up in some way. The woman was always naked, of course. Other times, he would try to hide the fact that he was looking at pictures and scenarios of sexual activities by switching screens when I walked in, or quickly picking up and strumming his guitar.

He continued to control every aspect of my life, and with the internet he became increasingly volatile in his mood and his actions. I would always do what he wanted out of fear and intimidation. We would be downstairs together, or in our bedroom while he was on the computer, and he would get angry at me if I wanted to go to another part of the house. He would literally order me to "stay" and to "sit back down, you are not going anywhere." I started to think about leaving him again, but it was such a big decision. Where would I go? How would I support myself? How would I keep a steady job? What would I do about money?

I decided, in my absolutely broken heart and soul, that this was just the way my life was going to be, and I should accept it as such.

That did not stop me from fearing him more and more. I knew that eventually he would slip and make his true intentions known. But when the words came out of his mouth, I was not at all ready. We were in our basement and he was working out on his weight machine. He worked out down there several times a week, and I always had to sit there with him until he finished. That night, we argued about something. I tried to run away, and he stood at the base of the stairs, arms outstretched, blocking the path. He said, "If you try to leave me, I will kill you." My heart stopped. I began to cry. He hated it when I cried — it seemed to send him somewhere outside of himself. "Stop crying, stop your fucking crying," he would scream. I was reduced to nothingness and sat back down on the couch with my head in my hands. He finished his workout and we went back upstairs together when he was done.

I had always thought he was capable of killing me, but after his outright threat to do so, I had no doubts at all.

# CHAPTER 9: THE FIRST ESCAPE

Paul carried a loaded weapon with him everywhere he went — a 40-caliber handgun. The gun was either in his car, in the garage, or, at other times, on the kitchen counter or his nightstand. Everyone who frequented our house — which was really only our children — knew that the gun was always within reach. They also knew that it was always loaded and ready to go. He would say, again and again, "If you ever need to use the gun, just point and pull the trigger — just point and shoot." He explained that the safety was never on, so it was easy to use if we ever needed to, for any reason.

With that continuing reminder — "Ready to go, just point and shoot," — I started to wonder if the ongoing abuse and purposeful wrecking of my mental and emotional health meant that he wanted me to kill myself. I started to believe that he was daring me, pushing me to do it. After all, he knew that I was capable of attempting suicide. He never said any words out loud to suggest such a thing, but it was obvious from his suggestions and intensifying abuse that he would not really care if I did just that.

I had had enough. I was ready to leave the marriage, or at least shake things up and let him know that the marriage needed to drastically change. Truthfully, I was not ready to divorce him and end it completely, but I did want him to know that I was not willing to put up with his blatant abuse. I needed to do something extreme to get his full attention.

So, I did it. I hired a moving truck and completely cleaned the house out of all of its contents. Both of my children, their friends, and some of my friends helped me accomplish this in a matter of a few hours. We were done and gone before he arrived home after work. I rented a storage unit for all of the household items, got them all tucked in, then took everyone who had helped me out to dinner. I had gone to my boss and gotten my paycheck two days early to make the move happen, and after paying for the moving truck, the storage unit, and dinner for everyone, I had no money left for anything, but I was free of him. I typed a letter to him and left it on the kitchen counter for him to find, explaining my actions. This is the letter verbatim:

July 6, 2004

Dear Paul:

This is probably one letter you will want to read entirely and not just "scan."

First and foremost, I loved you very much for a long time in our relationship, and I thought I would love you forever. You were my "knight in shining armor" so to speak, or so I thought. Here was my husband, big, strong, and handsome - and a police officer, a protector. I loved you so much, you always protected me, and in a way, you still do to this day.

I feel vastly different now. You have changed my love for you into resentment. You constantly insist that all of the things you do you do for me. Actually, you do them for both of us, and mostly the things you say you do for me you do to control me. I am tired of you doing for me what I can do for myself. You don't think you control me, but you do in many ways. I feel you have taken away who I am as a person, as an individual. You will never understand this because you can't see it. The same holds true for our "sex" life. You demand these certain things in return. You want me to dominate you when, in reality, you dominate the whole scenario. Because when you don't get what you want, life is miserable. You are angry with me 24/7, even if I do provide some type of pleasure for you. I can never live up to your expectations and, frankly, I don't want to. As you have said "I'm capable of better." Well, I'm not. I've come to the conclusion that you are impossible to make happy. I don't think you will ever find anyone that will make you happy. You say you love me, but I believe you don't really love me at all, or you would show me you love me through affection. I believe affection comes naturally. You are a very complicated person that not too many people understand.

According to you, it is always me that needs help, always me that needs to change. I feel stronger now than I have in a long time. I've taken a real hard look at myself, at my life. I need to start living as if each day is a gift and as if tomorrow were (sic) not to come. I am not doing that with you, am not doing anything with you except wondering what attitude you will have when you wake up or when you get home. I am constantly on pins and needles with a knot in my stomach. I can't live this way any longer. I honestly feel you need help Paul, you have many issues unresolved in your life that you need to deal with, and now another one. I don't think you love yourself, and therefore are not capable of loving anyone else. I also feel you need help with your sexual issues, I feel you are sick.

As you can see, I have taken what was mine and left some of what was mine for you. I took the dining room table and chairs and left the living room furniture for you. I have the van for now, I am assuming you will want it back. I am working on getting another car. I have left the bank card, and I have left my cell phone.

Please don't contact any of my family members. They are the only ones aware of what is happening, and I have shared with them the reasons I have left. Frankly, they all wanted to know why I stayed as long as I did.

I am truly sorry our relationship did not work. I feel like a total failure. No, I did not finish this marriage. No, I do not finish much of anything I start. And, no, it's not always my fault. I am sorry for the pain I have caused you, and I am sorry for the pain this will cause you, but I feel it is the best thing for both of us. I can't stay in a relationship I don't want to be in. I can't stay with someone I've come to resent.

It was a very nerve-wracking day, and I was fearful of how he would react. I was also relieved and proud that I had been able to take such a huge step. I had made plans to stay with my sister and her husband, but I had no idea what I was going to do in the future. It all depended on his reaction and whether he was willing to make some huge changes.

He called me immediately after he got home, absolutely devastated. I told him to leave me alone and not to call because I would not answer anymore. I told him I would call him when I was ready to sit down and talk. I kept my word and did not answer the phone. That did not stop him, though, from inundating my voicemail with messages at work — apologizing, crying, begging me to come back. He left messages at all hours of the day and night telling me how much he loved me and how much he cherished me as his wife. He begged me to not leave him alone and he promised to do whatever he had to do to make me happy. He promised to stop raping me and said he would get rid of all the sex items, if that was what I wanted.

After two or three days, I called and agreed to meet for dinner. I was shocked at how awful he looked — he seemed truly crushed. He was overly sweet and very caring, and he was teary-eyed during the entire meal. He was his like old self, the man I had first met and fallen for — charming and attractive, a nice guy. For the first time ever in our relationship, he brought me roses at work with a nice card attached. At least twice a week while I was gone, he sent roses. This was important to me because he did not believe in such sentiments — he had never bought me a gift for my birthday or any other occasion. He had never shown any appreciation or love in a giving way like that. In fact, we agreed at the beginning of our relationship that gifts were not necessary for any reason. Not that I ever really liked that idea, but it became clear over the years that he was incapable of these particular actions because he was incapable of giving. Anyway, I loved getting the roses, and he seemed to be genuinely reaching out. He implored me to give him a second chance, repeating that he loved me as his wife, and he did not want our marriage to end. He insisted that I was the best thing that had ever happened to him and he refused to let me go. He used God and quotes from the Bible, while assuring me that he was ready to be the husband that God wanted him to be. He said that I had been given to him as a gift from God. He said that he had abused the gift, taken it for granted, and that me leaving him was the exact thing that he needed to see the truth.

Over the next three weeks, he convinced me that he had, indeed, gotten the message. He asked me to meet him on

Sunday morning at church. He said that he had a special surprise in store for me and begged me to be there. I got to church and sat with my parents. I saw him come in and sit down. After a few songs and some announcements, the pastor called Paul up to the podium. The pastor explained that Paul wanted to speak to me in front of the entire congregation.

Paul stood up there and admitted that he had been abusive and controlling. He went on for several minutes, then asked for a prayer from the congregation for our marriage, that it be healed and restored. He then announced that he had a gift for me. He walked over, in front of everyone, and handed me a framed copy of 1st Corinthians, Chapter 13, entitled "Love" in the NIV version of the Bible. I accepted his gift. I believed everything he promised. That night, I went back home, and he hung the framed verse directly above our bed. It reads:

*1 Corinthians 13 —Love "1. If I speak in the tongues of men and of angels, but have not love, I am only a resounding gong or a clanging cymbal. 2. If I have the gift of prophecy and can fathom all mysteries and all knowledge, and if I have faith that can move mountains, but have not love I am nothing. 3. If I give all I possess to the poor and surrender my body to the flames, but have not love, I gain nothing. 4. Love is patient, love is kind. It does not envy, it does not boast, it is not proud. 5. It is not rude, it is not self-seeking, it is not easily angered, it keeps no record of wrongs. 6. Love does not delight in evil but rejoices with the truth. 7. It always protects, always trusts, always hopes, always perseveres. 8. Love never fails. But where there are prophecies, they will cease; where there are tongues, they will be stilled; where there is knowledge, it will pass away. 9. For we know in part and we prophesy in*

*part, 10. but when perfection comes, the imperfect
disappears. 11. When I was a child, I talked like a
child, I thought like a child, I reasoned like a child.
When I became a man, I put childish ways behind
me. 12. Now we see but a poor reflection as in a
mirror; then we shall see face to face. Now I know
fully, even as I am fully known. 13. And now these
three remain: faith, hope and love. But the greatest
of these is love."*

It was comforting to see God's words shining down on
me in the place where Paul had hurt me in so many different
ways, and I prayed that God would protect me. This gift,
this gesture of love from him to me, was a great statement;
one that I wanted to put all of my faith and all of my trust
in, but it would prove to be nothing but an empty gesture,
impossible for him to stand up to.

But for the first two or three weeks following my return
home he seemed like a changed man, and we were able to
communicate well about my requests and what I expected.
He seemed more spiritual and much kinder, and I believed
he was really trying to change. He agreed to get rid of all
of the sexual related items and said he would not come into
the bathroom with me and make me urinate into his mouth
anymore. He also agreed to give me more freedom to visit
with my family and my children. And he promised he would
stop demanding that I wait on him by providing all of his
meals at the post. In turn, he wanted me to be more loving
and attentive. He wanted me to come on to him more and
initiate sexual activities more often. He wanted me to make
him feel more wanted. I agreed to this request immediately.
I also tried to explain how he had made me feel worthless
and degraded with his sexual demands and increasing
violence. He admitted that he had acted inappropriately,

then he insisted that we pray about our problems and ask God to heal our marriage.

Within days, the bag of sexual items were gone, and, for a short time, things were truly different between us. At his request, he began praying out loud, with me in our bed, when we turned in for the night. He would actually pray that God remove his sexual demons and make him the husband he should be. He would refer to me as his precious gift from God and promise to love me and treat me as such. I felt remarkably close to him and believed that God would intervene and fix our marriage.

It was awesome while it lasted, but soon things were back to the usual. Slowly, methodically, all of his demands, expectations, and the sexual items came right back into our life. As it turns out, he had buried the bag of items in a deep hole on our property. Within a few short months, he dug them up and begged each and every one back into our marriage. He was unable to escape from his sadistic thoughts and actions. He said that he needed these sadistic activities to exist, that without them he was a closed-off, angry, completely discontented man.

It was at this very point that I, for the millionth time, suggested that he needed help. He agreed and said that he would see a psychologist. For several months we went individually and together as a couple. But it came to an abrupt end when I realized that our agendas were completely different. I wanted a loving, passionate relationship with mutual respect and affection and he wanted to turn his sadistic sexual desires into a lifestyle. He wanted me to give in, accept, and perform all of his demands and desires. He insisted that I would learn to love being his dominatrix if I could just open my mind and my heart. With a good, honest try, we could be a very happy married couple. He did not see anything wrong with his fantasies and believed that if I would simply cross over to his side, things would be good between us. It was obvious that he did not really believe he needed any help, in fact he thought it only made me look like a prude and an unwilling, resentful wife. We were again at an impasse without any compromise possible.

And, again, I was out of a job. Paul made it clear that he was fine with me being a non-working, always-at-home wife. Without the stresses of a full-time job, he said, I would have more time to be a good housewife. I would also have more time to concentrate on him and his needs and demands. There would be no more excuses about being overwhelmed or over-stressed. I was more than capable of focusing on my one reason to live — my one and only responsibility in life — him and what he wanted.

He presented this argument as such a blessing to me — he was freeing me of all of my outside troubles, leaving me plenty of time to rest, keep the house in order, and work on keeping my depression and migraine headaches in check. This was his compromise. This was his answer to our problems: He would give me free rein to do nothing but take care of him, his needs, his demands. It would be like a life of leisure for me, he said, and it would keep our marriage intact. He preyed upon my feelings of wanting to stay married, and not having to work was also an incredibly attractive offer. He had me in the perfect position and I caved right in.

Manipulation is an enormously powerful tool. Over time, in my own experience, it was life-changing. I really believed that my life was exactly as it was meant to be. I continued to convince myself that it "wasn't really that bad." I had a nice house and a nice car to drive, I had food, shelter, and clothing — everything I needed. Plus, I did not have to work anymore. He wasn't really that awful, was he? I believed in all of the condescending titles he put on me. I was a bitch, a prude, mentally sick and unstable, unable to make him happy, sexually, or otherwise, a bad wife, and it was only because of him that I was able to make it through each day. He had only ever given me one responsibility in our marriage, by the way, and that was to keep him happy and content sexually. Now he was making it impossible for me to fail by allowing me to not have to work. I fell right into the trap. Somehow, all of his control and manipulation had turned into brainwashing.

I realize that this may seem like a far reach to some of you. Lots of things seem like a far reach until you actually live it on a daily basis. Webster describes "brainwashing" as *"to indoctrinate so intensively and thoroughly as to effect a radical transformation of beliefs and mental attitudes."* Yes, exactly that. Of course, it was years later that I thought of calling it brainwashing. Today I can say, without any hesitation or disbelief whatsoever, that he brainwashed me. He was that good. Indeed, he was a true master at his craft.

Over the next several months, I allowed him to play me and control me in every way possible. I let him suck out all of the good and real qualities. I became exactly what he wanted me to be. And what was the outcome? His demands and his violence increased. I vividly remember lying in our bed one morning, after he had raped me, showered, and left for work. I was crying out loud and thinking to myself that he had made me his "sperm receptacle" — somewhere warm and moist to inject his poison into. That, for me, was a powerful realization because in my real heart and soul, I knew better. I knew that I was much more than that.

It is terribly hard to live with someone who constantly berates and criticizes you and everything you try to do. Someone who shows no love, compassion, or appreciation. Someone who turns you inward and ruins your self-esteem and confidence. I have always believed in the adage, "You are a product of your environment." The wonderful family I grew up with gave me the values I believe in today. But this environment, the one I lived in with Paul, was negative, uneasy, and tiring. I changed. I became a completely different person, unrecognizable to my old self. I loathed it. I loathed who I had become. I felt so dirty and nasty, having to do these horrid things to please him, these sexual acts with no feeling or emotion at all. I really felt like a whore. I realize how ironic it sounds for me to talk about being raped by my own husband, about feeling like a whore in my own bedroom. But that is exactly how it felt — degraded and filthy.

His ideas and his sick fantasies became more bizarre and out-of-the-question. For example, he wanted to bring a third party into our sexual activities, and he wanted me to be the one to decide exactly who that would be. I could choose a man or a woman, whichever I wanted. He asked me to consider going out to a bar, picking someone up, and bringing them home to our bedroom. I told him that would never happen. Why would he even consider putting me in such a position? I thought it was extremely dangerous. He did not agree with me about the danger, but I refused to talk about it, even after he had suggested it several times.

His next idea was even more odd, one that he almost begged me to make happen. He wanted me to go out and sleep with a man that I picked up in a bar, then return home to him so that he could suck that man's sperm out of me and clean me up. He preferred that the whole scenario happen from start to finish in our bedroom but said that if I were uncomfortable bringing another man home with me, he would be happy just cleaning me up. I refused to listen to this idea even more aggressively than the first. It made him angry, but I told him he was a sick bastard to suggest such a thing. I truly felt he had absolutely no respect for me as his wife, or even as a woman.

In fact, I would often point out to him that he did not respect me as his wife. He readily admitted that was true, and would say, "No, I do not respect you. Respect is earned." The other brilliant thing he felt compelled to remind me of was, "It is always easier for you to ask for forgiveness than it is for permission." I would get so angry and tell him, "Permission? I do not have to get permission from you to do anything." That, of course, was not the truth at all, and attempting to stand up to him by saying such a thing out loud really only made me feel worse about myself. I knew he had the first word and the last word. He made all of the decisions, no matter what. We both knew the truth. He decided everything; I decided nothing.

# CHAPTER 10: FEAR OF DEATH & DESTRUCTION

Our trips to Oklahoma to visit with his family occurred regularly, at least twice a year. Like my own parents, his mother and father had been married for over 50 years. We usually travelled to their house every Thanksgiving. I really liked it and got along well with all of them. I love them still today.

Paul was the oldest of the five children, and it was easy to see that he was the black sheep of the family. He was not really close to any of them, and they did not speak on a regular basis. A certain tension hung in the air when they were all together. I do not know exactly what it was about — I may never know — but it was not at all hard to recognize that something was not exactly right in his relationship with his immediate family members. It was obvious, but never discussed.

Over the ten years we were together, we would make that long trip — over twelve hours in the car — many, many times. He used to break the trip up into two days, which would allow us to travel only six hours the first day, stay in a motel for one night, then drive the remaining six hours the next day. There was no additional stopping for anything except a scheduled gas refill or a quick meal from the drive-through of a fast food place. He decided the where and when, of course.

He was also the one to decide if my visor was up or down. If I put it down because the sun was shining in my eyes, he was perfectly capable of reaching over and slamming it back up into place. He also refused to ride with the air conditioner on, insisting instead that all four windows be rolled down completely. Riding in a car for twelve hours with all of the windows rolled down is like being in a tornado. It was so loud with the wind whipping that you could not hold a conversation. Not that we had any discussions in the car. He was never interested in talking about anything other than sex and his sexual demands. And he absolutely refused to turn on the radio. I never rode in the car by myself without the radio blasting my favorite channel — doesn't everyone do that? — so this was particularly strange. We would often argue about it, and sometimes I would turn it on just to spite him, only to have him shut it off in disgust and remind me that I should be directing all of my energy and my thoughts on him. These car "rules" were always in force, no matter where we were going, even to get groceries or run errands. I always froze in the car too because he refused to turn the heat on anything but low, and he never, ever started the car in the driveway or in the garage to warm it up in the winter months.

Near the end of 2007, Paul's father became extremely ill and had a stroke. We travelled to Oklahoma then to see him in the hospital, and shortly after returning home, we were summoned back with the news that he would not live much longer. We drove back immediately and ended up staying for his funeral. This was a very sad time for Paul and his entire family, and it was one of the only times I ever saw Paul become humble and lose some of his arrogance.

On the day we were to return home, Paul went out to his parents' garage to go through some of his father's tools — his mother had given him permission to take what he wanted. He picked out some special items and packed them in the car. I happened to notice that one of them was a big, heavy mallet, about three feet tall and coated in rubber. I tried, but it was too heavy for me to lift without using both hands. It gave me a bad feeling and I wondered why he wanted it. He placed it on the floor, directly behind the driver's seat.

The mallet would be the topic of a discussion on the way home. "Why do you have that?" I asked. "What would you ever use it for?" His response, when it finally came, was quick and cold: "I'm going to use it to bludgeon you to death." My heart stopped. I felt like I was going to throw up and I began to cry. "Stop crying, you know I hate it when you cry, stop your fucking crying," he screamed at me. I could not stop crying, but when I looked over at him and saw the anger in his face, I choked on my crying just to shut up.

I remember the exact stretch of road that we were on. It was not the freeway; it was his short cut through the rural fields and farms and sparse woods of Illinois. I was filled with fear and horror. I was afraid that I might never make it home. I knew he could kill me and dump me anywhere, never to be found. But we always took this route, and I knew that we would be approaching a small gas station and store where we always stopped. I thought about getting out, running into the building, and screaming for help. But what would happen then? Would he become enraged? Would he laugh it off, claiming it was all a joke? I felt such a sense of pure dread. I was truly afraid for my life.

We did stop at that gas station, and I went in and used the bathroom and returned to the car without saying a word to anyone. The remainder of the trip was extremely tense, and I remember taking my cell phone out of my purse and putting it in the front pocket of my jeans so that I would have it on me in case I needed it. That incident was never discussed or brought up between us again, but it made me believe he had a definite plan in mind if he did ever want to end my life. I had no doubt that he was capable of killing me. I had no doubt that he would probably get away with it because of his police knowledge.

This was the second time he had threatened to kill me. It would not be the last.

# CHAPTER 11: BECOMING UNRECOGNIZABLE

There are so many more important facts that I need to tell you about, all of which happened in the last three years of our marriage. But I also need to admit that I cannot remember an exact timeline for when they occurred, or even in what order they occurred. Because of the state of my mind, my body, my emotions — my entire being — I was, for those last three years, silenced, squelched, unable to have real feelings, completely wrecked. I was just a shell of myself in all ways, from my demeanor to my actions and my skin and bones appearance. Trauma can affect your entire body and soul and shut your brain off in certain ways, sometimes to protect you without you even realizing it.

Anyway, I know that these things did actually happen, but exactly *when* escapes me, except that they all occurred between 2007 and 2009. And it's not that these particular events were any more or less tragic than the rest. It is just that they seemed to, somehow, tip the scale and make the pile of life-changing events so top-heavy that they finally had to come falling down.

The first of these is my daughter's wedding. Ashley had been with a young man for several years and they had produced my two beautiful granddaughters. The relationship was on and off and good and bad for its entirety, but I was happy when they decided to make their union official. They did not want a big, fancy affair, and they had planned on paying for what they could — along with help from her father and Paul and I. Ashley's great-grandmother offered to buy her wedding dress and they planned a nice ceremony with a big celebratory reception afterward with food, beer, and other alcohol. They also hired a deejay for the party — all the weddings in our family were always big, happy, dance parties.

I was excited that Ashley was happy and, after speaking with her father, we began to plan. I, of course, went to Paul to try and work out a budget that would fit with the events. Since I truly had no idea what our financial situation was, I made no outright suggestions about any amount and hoped that he and I could discuss this important matter sensibly. That plan would be nothing close to the reality. He made it clear that there would be no discussion whatsoever and that he did not care about any of the details. He did offer to make and provide any food that would be needed as far as side dishes. Then, he wrote me a check for $250.00, making it clear that that would be all he would be providing. I tried to explain how insulting this was, but he did not want to hear it. The wedding was not going to be a catered, sit-down dinner, but good food, drinks, and alcohol could cost several thousand dollars. I was working at the time and making decent money as I had agreed to fill in a few hours per week at a friend's law office while she looked for a full time assistant. Although I did not have access to any of our money or to the bank account itself, he made particularly good money and there never seemed to be a problem. We had a mortgage, a car payment, and other expenses, but I knew that our bills were always paid on time, and we seemed to have enough extra cash to eat our meals out often and keep groceries in the house.

I do not know why I was so surprised at his behavior — it was certainly nothing new as far as control and manipulation go — but I was particularly pissed-off and heartbroken. On my own, I went to the bank and borrowed several thousand dollars in my name, without telling him, and was able to provide Ashley with much of the money she needed to pay for part of her wedding. That was all I wanted.

Borrowing the money just to spite him was very wrong, and the fear and tension it caused me was awful, but I was tired of everything and it was my way of standing up to him. He, of course, eventually found out about it and was beside himself in anger. He felt I had disrespected him. I realize now that I was trying to hurt him and pay him back for all of the things he had done and was doing to me. I realize too, that I was very lost and reaching in the wrong direction to make myself feel better.

Ashley was the most beautiful bride ever, and the entire day was so special and shared by many loved ones. I spent the day at the church with her and her friends preparing for the event. Paul was to come later with his daughter, bringing the dishes we had prepared. With many helping hands, the meal turned out wonderfully with her father as the grill master, serving up pounds and pounds of fresh grilled pork, barbequed pork, plus all of the usual fixings. The drinking and the dancing were to begin around 9:00 that evening.

Paul did his best, in the weeks before the wedding, to let me know that we — meaning he, his daughter, and I — would be leaving early because he did not like the fact that people would be getting intoxicated and driving home impaired. He did not want any part of that with his position as a police officer. I knew what his real intentions were — he really just wanted to stop me from drinking or dancing and having any fun. Even worse, all of my attention would obviously be directed towards my daughter, the bride, and my family members and friends. He would do whatever he needed to do to make sure that he remained my top priority, even on my only daughter's wedding day.

I believe now that he formulated his plan weeks in advance because he knew that if he tried to "make" me leave that day in front of my family and friends, it would be war. He knew that he was not going to be able to suggest such a ludicrous thing on the day of the wedding. And he also knew that if he imposed his control at the event, it would be in the presence of my family and friends.

After many arguments and tears on the days leading up to the wedding, I was able to make it crystal clear that I would not be leaving early, that I would be dancing and having a drink or two to celebrate the occasion whether he liked it or not. I knew I could not, in any way, give in or bow down to his demand because if I showed him any cracks, he would pounce on me and break me. As it turned out, I stood my ground and remained steadfast in my position. He did, in fact, leave the venue right after dinner, sneaking out without saying a word to me or anyone else. His daughter was having a good time, and I knew that she wanted to stay and dance and have fun, but she was gone as well.

I felt stupid trying to explain to everyone where he had gone and why he had left so early, but I made no excuses for his behavior and simply described it as "Paul being Paul." No one was really surprised, and no one missed him either. I was on edge, however, and feared returning home to face my consequences. When I got home, I washed my face and crawled quietly into bed, only to have him say, "I know that you are home, I can hear you." That was it. Nothing more was said at all, and for the next several days he gave me the silent treatment. I did not care. I was over it. This would be one of the very few times I stood my ground, but I felt that my daughter deserved nothing less. I also knew in my heart that I was right, and any man who would even think of suggesting such a selfish thing was not only wrong, but unquestionably wrong. His daughter, by the way, expressed her disappointment in having to leave early to please him, but only to me privately.

\* \*

Paul's oldest daughter was the heart-wrenching subject of another important incident from this time. I had been present on only three occasions when Paul and his two older children were in the same place at the same time, and each occasion had been awkward and uncomfortable. One of those occasions was a funeral for Paul's ex-father-in-law. He invited me to go with him, and we drove over two hours to pay his respects. It was rather odd, however, because he insisted on wearing his uniform. He also got permission from his lieutenant to take a police car, something that he had never done before for any reason. The state police did not take police cars home or drive them without being on duty, but he felt strongly about making a statement. I always thought that the statement was really about how important he thought he was. He felt the need to rub his presence in his ex-wife's face — and in his ex-best friend's face since they were still married. I believe it back-fired on him because neither of his children acknowledged his existence until he was able to get his son to step outside. A loud conversation prompted our exit almost immediately. He did pay his respects to his ex-wife, however, and she was glad to see him there, I think. Paul never wanted to discuss his older children, and the incident with his son at the funeral was no different. He refused to talk about it at all. But I could see and feel the hurt he held onto and I knew it was hard for him. I think it crushed him and changed his attitude towards himself.

Then, sometime in those last three years, I remember him coming home from work saying that he had received an e-mail from his daughter. She was engaged and planning a wedding. Over the next several months, he would occasionally mention that he had spoken to her or heard from her about the details. Eventually, he asked her the obvious question — the question that seemed to consume him — and that was whether he would be giving her away to her husband at the wedding. She informed him that no, he would not be giving her away. She said she had decided at an incredibly young age that her mother would have that honor.

He was absolutely devastated by this news, but it did not take long for his feelings to change to anger. I do not know anything about their subsequent exchanges, as he was not willing to share any of that with me. I do know that once he realized that he would not be front-and-center as her father, he informed me that we would not be attending the wedding at all. He was not, he said, going to sit on the sidelines at this important event. And, since his daughter had put him in his place by denying him the right, he refused to even show up. I voiced my opinion in the matter, telling him more than once that we should definitely be there for her, but he would not entertain the thought. I was done bringing it up. He did not care about what I thought, anyway. And I knew that, for my own good, I needed to leave it alone.

When the invitation to the ceremony and the reception arrived in the mail, it was addressed to him and me and his youngest daughter. The wedding was going to be held in a neighboring state and included in the invitation was a list of available hotels and accommodations. He showed this information to me and I took advantage of the invitation to renew my thought that we should definitely show up for his daughter's big day. No, absolutely not, he said. That was the last time we would discuss the issue, period. He had made up his mind to not attend.

About three weeks after the wedding, I arrived home to find a box, delivered by UPS, which was addressed to him and sent by his daughter. I brought it into the house and put it on the kitchen counter. I never considered opening it, of course. He arrived home, saw it sitting there, picked it up, went to the bedroom, and closed the door behind him. I was curious to know the contents of that box, but knew enough to not intrude or inquire about it until he was ready to let me in.

Later in the evening, I went into the bedroom to do something. He was on the computer and the box was on the bed, opened up. It contained two dead corsages — still in their original plastic containers from the florist — and an empty 8" x 10" frame void of any picture. When I asked him about the box, he told me that it had also contained a note from his daughter explaining that the corsages had been there on the day of the wedding for us to wear. The frame would have contained a picture of her and her father on that special day — had we of shown up as she expected. The note was something he refused to show me, and following his quick explanation, he made it perfectly clear that he was done discussing it and not to ask any more questions. I was horrified for his daughter, but I left it at that. It was over, done.

I would find out the whole story years later, after I had been in prison for over a year, when much to my shock and wonderment, I received a letter from Paul's first wife. I will share more about our correspondence back and forth later in my story, but I want to tell you the story I heard about his daughter's wedding day now, as I learned it from her own mother.

As you can imagine, we had many things to share and many pressing questions to ask. One of the first things she wanted to know was why we had not attended the wedding. I immediately shared with her what had occurred: I told her about his disappointment at not being able to give his daughter away — which did not surprise her at all — and his subsequent decision not to attend. She, in turn, shared with me that Paul had informed his daughter the exact opposite — that we would indeed be there. She went on to tell me that the wedding ceremony started more than a half hour late due to the fact that she was waiting for us to arrive.

Paul's ex-wife then described what happened immediately following the ceremony. It made my heart cry out loud. She explained that right after the bride and groom walked back down the aisle as husband and wife, a member of the bridal party came to summon her to the bathroom. Her daughter had requested her presence. In the bathroom, she saw her newly married daughter standing there with a pair of scissors and a garbage bag. The daughter was holding her wedding veil, the veil her mother had also worn on the day she married her father. The daughter had hoped that her father would recognize it as such. But, having to come to terms with the fact that her own father had not bothered to show up on her special day, she told her mother to use the scissors to cut the veil in half, which was many feet long and trailing. The two of them could then throw the bottom half in the garbage bag to symbolize that they were "cutting him out of their lives forever." The photographer was present, at the bride's request, in order for them to have pictures of this momentous event.

I cannot even imagine the rush of emotions that must have been running through each of those women in that moment. The entire day must have been very disappointing and draining. And I cannot come up with any excuse for Paul's reasoning in this matter. Somehow, I am sure he was able to put the blame on me as to why we did not attend his daughter's wedding. But I assure you that it was out of my control. He made that decision. He put that dark cloud over his own daughter's special day. He and he alone.

Being apprised of this unfortunate event years after my own traumatic experiences only elevated my sincere hatred for the man. He truly did enjoy inflicting pain, in any way possible, on the people he claimed to love.

# CHAPTER 12: THE IMPENDING FIRE

At some point during these last three years his youngest daughter came to live with us on a permanent basis, only visiting with her mother for a few weeks in the summer. Because of that, Paul was gone from the house much more, as he insisted on being involved in every aspect of her life as far as school and church activities. Suddenly, I was not his only focus. He began going places and doing everything with her. I was expected, of course, to go along and join them, but there were so many days when I was barely able to get out of bed. I was consumed with headaches, depression, and fear. And all of the interactions I had with Paul were stressful, confrontational, or abusive.

The activities in the bedroom, however, were ongoing. New things, more sadistic and frightening things, were constantly being added to our "sessions." He had always really liked it, for example, when I smothered him and made it hard for him to breathe. At certain times in the past, he had attempted to do the same thing to me. He would hold his hands over my mouth and nose or hold my face up tight against his chest as he lay on top of me. I would kick and squirm and try to free myself. I would ask and plead with him to stop. He would never take it too far or try it too often. It scared me to death and usually ended with me crying.

Now he began smothering me more frequently. He would put his hands behind my head and press my face against his chest during intercourse. Supposedly this action helped him achieve or intensify his orgasm — which was also the reason that he liked me to smother him. But he seemed to get a different feeling by doing it to me. I did not like it at all. He also attempted to suffocate me by putting a pillow over my head and holding it there, with me screaming, kicking, and sweating. I remember begging him to please never do that again. I was angry and scared.

His other new obsession was anal sex, something that had only ever occurred twice before. I had told him then that I hated it, that with his piercings it was very painful and uncomfortable. He had not mentioned it for a long time, but now it was suddenly what he had to do. The other two times had not been forceful, it was done slowly and somewhat considerately. But now his intentions were deliberate, violent, and against my wishes. He began raping me anally and there was no reasoning with him. There were times that I would bleed for days afterwards. This act made me feel like he really hated and despised me. I was becoming more and more fearful of him.

It seemed that his intentions and his desire to hurt me were elevating. I needed to get away from this man for good, somehow, or I would be dead. I knew this in my gut like I know my own name. Anything I had ever heard about domestic abuse, and the elevation in the abuse, told me that death was imminent.

I did it again. I left him for the second time. And this time was different in every aspect in that I truly feared him and believed he was going to eventually kill me. I needed to get away and figure out how to stay away.

I emptied the house of its contents, as I had done before, but this time I found a small house to rent and I moved in within a few hours. Something else I did was call the state police post a couple of days prior to moving out, on a day that Paul was not working and was not at home either. I spoke to his lieutenant and I told him that I was leaving the home. I asked him to please make sure Paul stayed at the post on a particular day, moving day. I said that I feared he would come home and catch me in the act of leaving him. I really do not remember too much about that conversation, but I do know that I told his boss that our marriage was in bad shape. I know that I told him that I was afraid of Paul. The lieutenant was genuinely nice, and he assured me that he would keep Paul busy at the desk and make sure he did not leave the post. Thinking back now about that telephone call, I wonder what the lieutenant really thought. I wonder if he was concerned about my fear of Paul. I was aware that everyone Paul worked with had heard more than once that I was sick, so sick that I could not take care of myself and needed help to survive each day.

So, again, I was gone. And this time I had every intention to stay gone and move forward with my life, although I was also aware that my ability to keep myself going was compromised by my mental and emotional state. I reached out to a past co-worker from my days at the courthouse who was now working as a counsellor at the local women's shelter, and she encouraged me to come to the shelter where we could figure it all out. I was very torn about taking this avenue, however, because of Paul being a police officer — I really did not want him dragged through the muck and felt sick at the thought of our marriage becoming a headline or a news story locally. I would try to fix it myself. Just getting away from him was a huge step in the right direction.

Again, even at this critical juncture, no one knew — I had not told anyone what was happening to me at his hands. I do not believe that I was fully aware at that time of the totality or the urgency of the scenario. I was numb, doubtful, and incapable of coming to terms with reality. It was much easier to diminish and lessen the acts, the abuse, and even easier to pretend they were not occurring at all. Of course, my continued refusal and denial that I was being abused in every way imaginable, that I was "just fine," could not have been further from the truth. But I kept pushing it down further and further into a dark hole in my soul and hoped that, somehow, I could overcome this one obstacle that was preventing me from living or moving forward. Even so, I was really unsure of my ability to start over on my own. I was not feeling well at all, emotionally or mentally. I felt that I was running scared. I had no plan and I really did not have the money or resources to do what I was doing. I was living on hope and prayers. But I knew beyond a shadow of a doubt that I needed to get away from him. And I got away, but staying away became a completely different hurdle.

When Paul realized that I was gone, he reacted exactly as he had the first time. He was devastated, beside himself, wrought with helplessness. He called me over and over on the phone. I explained that I would not tell him where I was, and if he did not stop contacting me, I would get a restraining order. Even worse, I would go directly to his lieutenant for his assistance in the matter. That last threat was more than enough to stop his calls. It would take two or three days before he was able to re-group and come up with an entirely different plan of attack.

Which, of course, he did. I had started working for an attorney who was assisting me and providing the support I needed to pay my expenses. I began receiving letters at work, ten days in a row, from Paul. These letters were typed and signed, "Love, me," in pen. Each one of these letters was addressed, not to me by my name, but to "Beautiful." They were full of apologies and kind words and prayers directed to God about fixing our marriage. Here are his written words to me:

*"I can reflect and guess all I want about this. I am not going to. As I have told you many times, I spoke from my heart. Many times, the word No came from my mouth. In my prayers, God now continues to remind me my answer is "yes" and "amen." And, he has shown me my uncountable errors with his word.*

*Beautiful, you are the most beautiful person I have ever looked at. You make me so happy in so many ways you will never know. I may not always show it, believe me it is absolutely true. There is no other person in this world I want to be with. You turned my life to the Lord, to start with. You allowed me to be open and honest with my feelings and emotions. You gave me love and trust. Don't ever believe anything else. My mouth is my worst enemy. I cannot take back the things I have spoken in the past. I can only promise to learn to control the words I use. It will be hard because many times I do not even know what I said or how I said it. This is where I need help. I have asked God for temperance to remove the fire in my words, to be humble not cutting, to praise not demean, to honor not discourage. I ask you to make me the better man I need to be to care for, protect, honor, respect, cherish and love my wife. I am not perfect Lord. I understand my errors and need to change. I accept my downfalls and ask for your forgiveness. Please empower me with the knowledge I need to complete these changes. Guide me through to be a better man, father, and husband to the wife I so dearly love. I ask you to please come home. This is the house we built for us, no one else. There is no money in our home, just the two lives it contained covered with God's grace and love. Continue to fill my heart with the Holy Spirit as I can (sic) continue this fight against the devil who comes to steal my wife, kill our spirits and destroy our marriage. In your word, I fight this battle. I take refuge under the power of your word. Devil you shall not win this battle. I cast you under our feet. You will not dwell in us. Lord, as the days grow longer and the time apart greater, we ask for strength and guidance. You allowed us to wed under your Holy name. We pray you keep your gift together. Tell us how to repair the wreck we have made. Do not allow this marriage to be destroyed. We have failed before and before. We do not want to fail this time. We honored ourselves in our words of never leaving each other. Lord, give us direction. Lead us to where we need to be. Let us find forgiveness with each other and ourselves. Calm our hearts and steady our souls. We know we love each other. Let us find this warmth and devotion again. Allow us to honor, respect and cherish each other. Lord continue your work in me. I know I am a long way from the man you seek in me. Let me grow and understand. Let me show the love and romance I have in my heart for my wife without fear. Let it pour out and spill upon Joni covering her as she so much wants from me. Lord, break this stronghold in my life. Let me give freely without fear or rejection and resentment. Remove this fear that binds me so tightly. Lord, we pray for restoration in our marriage. Protect it Lord - let it not fall into the hands of the evil one. Lord, continue your work in me. I feel your presence and guidance. Lead me Lord, I am yours. Break these binds that surround me. Let me overcome my rigidness and fear of rejection. Let me conquer the fears so I can be a better man, father, and husband to my wife I love so deeply. Lord, give my wife the courage to honor her words of never wanting to be divorced again. Let her feel the love in our marriage. Let her accept your words. Let her fight for us and continue to humble and correct me for my horrible errors. Lord, I cannot stand in front of you with my wife as you have directed. I will present her to you Holy as you direct. Let us stand before you and recommit ourselves to you in a blessed marriage ceremony approved by you. Let us profess our love and dedication to you in a house of worship. Lord, I feel my wife's heart deep within me crying for help. Grant her wish, Lord. I am not with her and cannot give her what she needs now. Allow her to see all the good within and none of the bad. Let her judge fairly us as your married couple and not as individuals. Give her the strength to step past any and all things yielding her from returning to your great gift of marriage. Let her honor her words of never wanting to divorce. Let me honor her with change, respect and protection. Destroy my fears which bind me. Joni and I pray for forgiveness. We have done many things wrong and ask for your mercy. Lord, I have searched my heart and accepted those changes needed to make myself the husband I need to be in the eyes of my wife. For me to love my wife, I must romance her like the first time I saw her. It shall be done. You have crushed the fear of rejection out of me. I will hold her hand like the budding groom who has just been married to his bride. I will kiss her with passion as if it were our last kiss. I will present her to all as my beautiful wife. I will give her the things she needs to know I really do care about her. My mouth is sealed from vial (sic) announcements and questions. I will honor her as the most beautiful person I have ever seen. I will protect, comfort, aid and love her with all my being. She must be allowed to grow in all areas never restricted by any of my actions. Lord, my wife has the most complete and honest trust in all she does from me. I will never doubt her again. For as much as I may trust myself, I must trust her. Lord, all the evil of my demented sexual thoughts and acts I cast out. It is gone from me forever. How wrong could I have been?? What a fool I was. It was not love, nothing more than a twisted act of the devil. How can I love or be loved?*

*Let my wife destroy anything she possesses related to this. It is banished from our lives forever. I will love my wife the way you intended and No (sic) other way. This I do for my wife, me and our marriage. Devil, you do not have a hand in this anymore. I am free, Oh God, I am so free. Thank you, Lord, thank you. Lord, let my wife take this to heart. I was once a fool and I am No (sic) more. I hurt my wife so badly, I ask for her forgiveness. Lord, I ask for your forgiveness. Lord, you have cleansed me of this wickedness FOREVER. Lord, I thank you for your power and vision. Beautiful, I feel so wonderful and free with this. You must believe me, this is gone, never to return. You will NEVER hear about any of this again. This is my ABSOLUTE best prayer. What a revelation from GOD. I have been released from the most harmful aspect of our marriage. Test the waters and find out. I end this as I will until this is over. This is my broken heart passionate plea to you to please find it in your heart the strength to not let our marriage be destroyed and end. No questions, just total acceptance with arms wide open."*

I have read these letters from him several times over these past few years but rewriting them to include in my story has been draining and gut-wrenching. Everything he says in these letters were truly everything I wanted from him and with him. I wanted so badly to believe that he was capable of his words. But I had severe doubts, and my intuition was screaming loudly to stay strong and, more importantly, to stay away.

The next several weeks would be hell. My family members and my children knew exactly where I was, and I knew that Paul would eventually find me, using all of the tools at his disposal. I began seeing state police cars drive by my house at all times of the day and night. Several times, he even pulled into my driveway. He had turned into a stalker — a stalker with a badge and a gun.

It was Christmastime, and after receiving his letters and not responding over a period of about three weeks, a box was dropped off at my parents' house. I picked it up but decided to wait and open it when I arrived at home. It was a really strange package — an empty cereal box wrapped entirely in masking tape — and I was not sure what it contained. It was very heavy.

My son was at the house when I returned — he had come to spend the night with me — so I took the box into the kitchen and opened it privately. The box contained the pottery trivet that I had inadvertently left on top of the stove. It was about eight inches in diameter and was used to hold spoons while cooking. Paul had taken the large, round piece of jewelry out of its piercing on the end of his penis and super-glued it to the middle of the trivet. I was caught off guard and appalled. I could not understand the meaning behind it. There was nothing else in the box — just this sick, confusing, very weird gesture.

I cried out loud while trying to explain to my son what, exactly, was glued to the middle of the trivet. Both of my children knew that Paul had a pierced penis — and they unanimously agreed about how sickening it was. They also knew that both of his nipples were pierced because they had seen him walk around the house without a shirt.

I, of course, had to call Paul then, to try and find out what he was thinking with that stunt. He cried and begged me to meet him for dinner. He said he had a real gift for me. I refused to meet him, but within a few days he was at my front door begging me to let him. I did, and we sat on the couch where he proceeded to present me with a gold, three-diamond wedding band. This was very unlike him. Gifts were not exchanged in our relationship, not for any reason.

I was hesitant; it did not feel right at all. I know he read the doubt in my face.

But we talked about the letters, and he insisted that he really was a changed man. He insisted that he did not want our marriage to end. I asked him again why he had sent me that "package," and he said he wanted to prove to me that he was trying very hard to change his sexual character into something I would be happier with, something more the way that God wanted. He was sure that if he sent his piercing ring to me, I would know he was trying and willing to change. He begged me to come home and suggested that the diamond ring could be part of a marriage renewal service that he wanted to have in November of the next year to celebrate our tenth anniversary.

I was feeling uncomfortable, having him in my house, and I told him that I would think it over and get in touch with him in a few days. After asking him many times to please leave and give me some time to think, he finally did.

I was overwrought with emotions, most of them on the negative side. Although I wanted to believe his intentions were real and true, I could not. His explanations about the trivet had not done anything to change my belief that the gesture was nothing more than a sick, demented "something" with maniac written all over it. I did not sleep at all that night or the next day. I did not go to work either. I finally decided to contact him and give the ring back. I wanted to let him know it was over for good.

How was I going to do this, though? I did not feel like I could face him and give him the ring back without having other people close by. I was afraid of how he would react, and the usual feeling, the expectation and dread of not being able to predict his state of mind took a first and foremost priority spot. This not knowing, this trying to guess what his mood or reaction would be at any given time was something I struggled with on a daily basis. I could never predict what he would be like, whether he was coming in the front door or a room at the house. It was not that he was extremely up or extremely down — it was his unhappiness, discontent, his constant disgust with anything and everything. It was the degree in which these emotions could change and the short amount of time in which that could happen. He was completely unpredictable in his actions and in his mind-set.

I was very confused. I was fearful to be with him, yet I was even more fearful to leave him. I was between the proverbial rock and a hard place. My decision to stay or leave would prove to be life-changing at this critical juncture. I knew the correct answer in my very being, and my entire circle of family and friends agreed that leaving him was the only answer. They all felt this way based strictly on things that they had seen or experienced firsthand. They knew absolutely nothing of the totality of his abuse, control, and manipulation. Had any of them known even a small part of any of it, or if they had known about his threats to take my life — then what?

I made what would turn out to be the wrong decision. I drove to the local sheriff's department. I did not personally know anyone who worked there, but I walked in and asked if I could speak with a sergeant or someone else in charge. I told them that I was Paul's wife, and that I needed to speak with someone about an urgent matter. Almost immediately, they escorted me into the office of the sheriff himself. Just like that, we were alone in his office, with no one else present or even knowing I was there.

I think back now to that day and realize, with the assistance of years of healing, that I could have used those few minutes to change the entire course of my story. But I was still incapable of reaching out for help. All I could do was explain to the sheriff that I needed to have something of importance delivered to Paul at the state police post. I asked if he could assist me in getting that accomplished. I remember being vague in my answers to his pointed questions, but I am sure he knew I was fearful.

Unable to get much information or any details from me, the sheriff said that his office could not (would not) help me, due to the sensitive nature of my request. However, he would be willing to contact the state trooper who worked in the immediate area and I could ask for his assistance in the matter. I knew this trooper personally — Paul was his sergeant, and that knowledge sank like a rock. I knew that I had made a huge mistake by reaching out to any law enforcement agency.

But the sheriff got the trooper on the radio, and he phoned the department to speak with me. I felt totally stupid at this point — on top of all of my other emotions — and although the trooper was very nice and shared my concern, he made it clear that he would not get in the middle. "Come on, Joni," he said. "Paul is my boss and I do not want to be involved in this." He went on to say something along the lines of not wanting to be "put in this position," as he felt it would reflect badly on him. I did understand his concern, and that only cemented the acknowledgement that I had made a big mistake. The trooper then encouraged me to give the ring back myself, assuring me that it would be fine. I am sure that he wondered why I felt I could not do this by myself, but I also believe that no one on this particular day wanted to ask too many questions. Unwilling to open up the entire can of worms, I was still able to pierce the top of the can just enough where more than enough shit fell out. Enough to deter any of them from wanting to get involved in any way.

It is ironic to me now, as I recall this incident to write it down, knowing as I do that the end result of this scenario could have been completely different had this particular incident taken a different course. Please realize that I do not blame anyone but myself for this irony. None of these professional, well-respected law enforcement officers could have possibly known, or even fathomed, the truth about this man who was my husband. Without me opening my own mouth to bring it to light, without asking for help because of the intricacies I perceived surrounding the entire thing, it would only be a matter of time before the whole situation would explode like a bomb.

When situations become so big and so overwhelming, to the point in which they have to blow up, it makes sense that anything and everything close to or connected to that explosion implodes and falls into themselves as a predictable consequence. My actions would cause my family, my friends, the police force, and so many other people to implode and collapse inward. There would be pain and disbelief all around.

But more things would need to happen before the explosion, each one adding more fuel and ammunition to the coming fire.

# CHAPTER 13: THE MATCHES ARE READY

I left the sheriff's department feeling completely defeated and drove directly to the state police post. I remember physically shaking as I parked and walked in quickly and caught Paul's attention. He was surprised and happy to see me walk in the door, but his elation did not last but a few seconds when he saw my face and the tears falling from my eyes. I asked him to meet me outside, then turned on my heels and went back out the door. He ran outside after me, asking me what was wrong, wondering why I was so upset, pleading with me to say something. I was crying in that gut-wrenching way, like when you feel sick to your stomach and want to throw up. I could not catch my breath; no words would come out of my mouth. Finally, I just handed him the box containing the ring and cried, "Take this. I don't want it." I begged him to "Just let me go." "I'm done with this," I said. He was speechless and tried to kiss me, but I got away from him and into my car and drove away. He ran beside the car as I pulled away, crying. I could see the pain in his eyes, and I remember wondering why he had never shown this much emotion to me before.

Over the next couple of days, he tried several times to call me, but I refused to answer. I had seen a different kind of desperation in him when I gave him the ring back, and I was consumed with fear that he would show up at my house or do something drastic or crazy in some scary way. Therefore, I was, to say the very least, absolutely shocked when a process server — someone I knew very well — showed up at the law office where I worked to serve me with divorce papers. Yes, I was shocked at this action by him, especially after all of his kind words and hopeful prayers about not ending our marriage and how much he was trying to change to be able to love and cherish me forever. It seemed like such a stark contrast to all of his efforts over the past six weeks. But I accepted it and prepared a response to the divorce complaint.

Meanwhile, other problems were raising their heads. As I continued to work for the woman attorney in her one-practitioner firm, it became impossible not to notice her lack of clientele. Then, there was the negative balance in her checking account, together with the onslaught of bounced checks and loan payment late notices inundating the daily mail. I spent a long time putting her past-due bills in alphabetical order at her request, and I was concerned about how she was going to pay the wages that were due to me in three days' time. I was already worried about how I was going to pay my bills and keep my head above water even with the paycheck — and now the security of the job was melting away as well. Here was another position I had never imagined myself in, especially in my mid-40s. I was attempting to start a new life with no money at all, a third divorce pending, and no solid employment.

Even worse than these harsh facts, I was an emotional and mental wreck. I had pushed down and buried deep inside my soul all of the abuse and sexual violence that I had survived. But I knew all too well that things buried deep within only grow deep, established roots and eventually begin to rot and disrupt your entire well-being. The rotting had already started, and I was depressed about my chances of making it through this challenge with all of these handicaps. On the other hand, though, I could feel a storm beginning to rage within myself.

Deep down, I knew I would eventually see the real man, the Paul who had been attempting to hide behind his nice words, his wishes to be a better man, to love and cherish his wife, etc., etc., etc. Sure enough, with the filing of the divorce papers, his attorney included a letter informing me that her client would be stopping all payments on the car that I drove, on the insurance premiums for the coverage of that car, and any and all other monies he paid out on a monthly basis to me for any reason. Of course, my name was not on any title to anything we owned together, and his decision to leave me with nothing until the settling of the divorce was solid.

I consulted the attorney I worked for, and she assisted me in creating a motion to file with the court, asking for interim spousal support based on our nearly ten-year marriage and his complete control of our finances. (I should say I assisted her in the creation of that document since she was the juris doctor and I was just her secretary/assistant.) Unfortunately, the threat of filing that document from my counsel to his, via a telephone call or two, was enough for him to go all the way to shut me down. His fear of paying spousal support plus the possibility of me bringing the face of the real man into a court fight, resulted in him shutting off my cell phone service. He knew that this would be the final blow, that it would bring me to the end of my rope, and that the fall was a truly short one. I was now unable to call my children, my family members, or anyone in my inner circle. This last shot of his was a bullseye.

I went home and added it all up: no money, no paycheck, no support. I left the house to go to the local phone store to see about getting a new cell phone in my own name but had to come to terms with the fact that they needed more than $400.00 to make this possible. I let go of the end of my rope. I went back home, took a long, hot bath, and cried myself to sleep. The next morning, I went to the law office to gather my personal belongings. I left my boss a note saying that I was quitting my job and that I would be in contact about the money she owed me. I knew all too well I would never see a penny of it.

I felt completely lost and out of touch with my life, and after several days of a million and one things occurring and me not really being mentally present for any of them, I found myself sitting on the couch in my rented house right next to Paul.

Again, as before, he was sweet and kind and full of promises. He apologized for filing for divorce and shutting off my phone, insisting that he just did what his attorney advised. He said, in fact, that he had never wanted a divorce at all and that he would immediately stop the proceeding. He said he would have my phone turned back on right away. He would pay my landlord any amount of money necessary to break my lease. He would help me move back into our house as quickly as possible.

He said all of the things he knew I wanted to hear and pushed all of the buttons he had so ingeniously placed within me through his abuse, control, and manipulation. I was putty in his hands. Once again, he was able to mold and soften me into making me believe that he was right, I was wrong. That he would care for me and provide for me.

Who was this person, this man who could manage each and every element of my life and well-being to such perfection? Perfection, that is, for him. He convinced me that not only was he the best thing for me, but he was the one and only thing I needed to survive. I felt as though he completely controlled my mind and my thoughts — not the best case scenario for solving problems, but the only scenario available to me at this critical time. I could have called for help by contacting my parents, my siblings, my children, or one of my friends; but since I continually insisted on going back to him, they felt their hands were tied. Yes, they were all angry with me for returning to the relationship over and over, but without knowing or understanding all of the horrid details, they clung to the belief that I was just trying to make my marriage work. And, since I was not in any way prepared to sit down and begin the process of spilling out all of my trauma and fears, my friends and family were comfortable keeping their distance.

I was somewhere I had never imagined, and the consequences of speaking out only led to more unknown traumas and fears. The situation was outside of my abilities of decision or understanding. I do not think I could even recognize the real, true nature of what, exactly, was happening to me. And I just could not get anyone else involved in this inexplicable, unbelievable, tumultuous situation.

Obviously I know now, all of these years later, with the ability to look back and evaluate, that I was in the deepest part of his cesspool, and that he was in the final stages of pushing me under in order to take every last piece of me.

That 20/20 hindsight thing again. I realize now that it does more harm than good feeding and keeping alive the hurts and trauma, re-opening wounds that bleed and scar, again and again. I may not ever be able to stop reliving it, but my tenacity to keep trying will never escape me. I do know for sure, however, that when the time comes for me to leave prison to start my life over again, believing in myself will be the key that allows me to move forward, look ahead, and thrive. I hope that my need to look back will diminish without the constant reminders. Yesterday, today, tomorrow, the minute I open my eyes in prison I am living the consequences of my decision. I am reliving the events that led to that decision and the actions I took to end the chaos in my life once and for all. Someday, maybe it will all be in the past where it belongs.

* *

I find myself getting way off track while I am trying to tell my story, and my mind wanders to being home again. This, too, shall pass. All bad things eventually do when they are driven by hope and prayers.

# CHAPTER 14: BACK TO HELL

I went back to that house and its toxic, life-sucking environment. I went back to everything as it had always been — like the rape, vaginally and anally, under the 13th chapter of 1st Corinthians. It hung on the wall directly above the horrific acts intentionally inflicted upon me. He had succeeded in making me believe I was ugly, mentally sick, a sexual prude, and a worthless and insignificant human being. He reminded me constantly of how "altruistic" he was, as a husband and a person. Ever since I had first met him, he constantly told me how loving and caring and giving he was, almost as if he were trying to convince himself. I had begun to disagree with him whenever he started boasting about all of his endearing qualities. I admit I was not being a very nice person myself. But in my worst moments, while enduring his abuse and control, I do not believe I ever came close to his level.

He would sit on the edge of our bed for hours at a time, talking "at me," not to me. He would use his powerful and authoritative tone to make me get up out of bed to take a shower. There were many times when he would physically remove me from bed and put me in the shower where I would cry until the hot water ran out. Then, he would dry me off, insist that I get dressed and wait outside in the running car for me to join him to go wherever it was that he wanted to go. He refused to let me marinate in all of my misery. I suppose that was actually a good thing, due to the fact that I did feel much better out of the house. But once we were home, in that house of evil, negativity, and blatant abuse, I was right back in bed. It became clear to me after several months that he was only making me get out of bed and on the road because he knew I would feel better, eventually, and he would be able to use and abuse me sexually when we returned home.

I think that what he really wanted was for me to break down completely. It is so odd, because I know he cared about me to some extent, but his true hatred for my unwillingness and my inability to meet his sexual demands trumped any positive feelings by leaps and bounds. I could see this softer, more caring side from time to time, but it was always quickly overshadowed by his unhappiness and discontent, almost as if he could not control himself or his actions.

Things began to get worse. The obvious decline in my mental health just made him more discontented. And even though he had dismissed the divorce proceeding, his unhappiness was apparent. He began acting out his anger by accelerating his verbal and emotional abuse. This pushed my fear into overdrive, and I made a concerted effort to please him in any way I could. During one verbal argument, he smashed his fist into the oak cupboard and bloodied his knuckles, which then left bruises. His insistence that I cause him pain during sex became worse. It was harder and harder for me to satisfy him sexually.

We were still attending church together, but I had stopped showing up two hours before the actual service while he practiced with the music praise and worship team. He was very annoyed when I stopped going early with him, but even more annoyed when I stopped going to church altogether. I was having a hard time because of his insistence that we walk in together, hand in hand, with him acting like the loving, supportive husband. I knew the real man and the truth behind his façade. I felt like he was mocking me. He wanted everyone to see him as the powerful, helpful police officer-husband looking out for his sick wife. The entire scenario sickened me, and I decided to remove myself from that part of his deceit.

As the status quo continued in our house, I became more depressed and began to lose any hope that things would get better. I decided that I needed to give up and get used to the way my life had turned out. I convinced myself that this was just the way it was going to be, and I tried hard to concede and accept it. Once again, I was not working and spent my time making a strong effort to make him happy, in any way possible, and most importantly, liking it. I knew that I would have to compromise myself and some of my beliefs, but I was willing to give him as much as I could since all of the other options had failed miserably.

It was like a tug of war within myself, and more times than not my real, true feelings and values won the fight. Besides, any effort I put forth went unnoticed and unappreciated, anyway. While he was busy with his job, his daughter's track team as an assistant coach, and teaching his daughter about music and playing the guitar, I became the least important person in his life — except as his sexual target. His anger and his aggression towards me were constant, but he certainly knew how to turn on his "good, caring husband" routine when other people were paying attention. I felt used and abused and unimportant and insignificant. He pretty much cemented that feeling one day when I was trying to talk to him about how disconnected I felt, how used by his sexual depravities. He did not want to hear about my thoughts or feelings and made it clear that I was around for only one reason: sex. He did try to make me feel special in that I was, at least, able to do that for him. So, I was his sexual toy, his personal sperm receptacle. He could do as he wished to me because, in his opinion, I had not earned his respect as a wife or partner. He ended the discussion by telling me that I was not intelligent enough to hold a conversation with him about anything of consequence. I should have felt privileged to be his wife because he was so special and so important.

And angry and volatile. I never knew exactly what his attitude towards me was going to be when he came home from work. I became much more conscious about making sure things were "just so" before he was due home. I wanted to make sure there was nothing to displease him or send him into a rage. After folding clothes or cleaning, I found myself turning off the television to wait for him in the kitchen, or sometimes just sitting quietly on the couch, getting ready to turn all of my attention on him when he came in the door. That was what he expected. I made sure I was never on the phone when he came home because that, in itself, was enough to harden and ruin his attitude. My children knew there was trouble because if I was talking to them on the phone and said, "I have to hang up, Paul is home" or "I will call you back later, now is not a good time," the conversation was over. I was running interference out of fear at what he might do, never really being sure what might set him off. It was to the point where my children would only come to see me when he was not there — calling ahead to check on his whereabouts.

I will try to explain the overwhelming feeling that I had each and every time he arrived home. Imagine getting pulled over by the police. It has happened to everyone for one reason or another. You might be in a big hurry, or late for work or an appointment. You drive too fast or run through a yellow light. Suddenly, you notice a police car in your rearview mirror. Your thoughts immediately change from "being late" to the situation at hand. You pray he doesn't activate his lights and siren. You feel sick to your stomach and start to sweat. You cannot take your eyes off of his car, following you. He turns on the siren and the lights. Your hands are clammy. You wonder, *Will he be nice, or will he be an asshole? Will he saunter up to the car with all of his power, authority, and control just to scare me?*

*What will he ask me? How should I respond?* It's a moment of "Oh shit" that makes you feel dizzy and sick. You have absolutely no control over what is about to happen. You are at the officer's mercy. He is in complete control and there is nothing you can do to stop him — outside of committing a felony, of course.

These are the exact feelings I had for years when I expected him home. It would start with the sound of the garage door going up automatically as he came up the long driveway. That sound, that soft humming of the motor, made me feel sick and nervous with anticipation. I was immediately afraid. Afraid of what he would do, afraid of his attitude and his presence. This is no way to live a life, and I lived this way for far too long. I had tried so many times to escape him, all to no avail. I was stuck in this relationship and I was at a loss as to how to be free.

I have reached out to many professional people in my life: my physician who kept me well, my psychiatrist who treated me for many years, even some women I knew in the mental health practice. Once, I attempted to talk to one of my best friends about where I was in my life but was unable to speak about the truth of the matter and let the abuse be known. I did not have the strength or the knowledge to bring it to the forefront. I know now that this is common for women in the claws of an abuser, and it is an incredibly sad and tragic effect. We become silent, unable to speak, unable to act in our own best interests. Strong women become weak, and weak women become invisible. We are dominated and swallowed up with shame and we surrender ourselves completely to our abusers. We are non-existent and unrecognizable to ourselves and to others. We are the worst kind of victim — we have no feelings of any kind; we are complete emptiness and vulnerability.

It was April of 2009, I think, and I was drowning in my own emptiness and vulnerability. Paul had threatened my life again after I had said that I wanted to "leave and stay gone and never see him again." He stood up, pointed his finger in my face and stated, "If you even try to leave me again, you won't make it out the door alive." I heard that loud and clear, but mostly I felt it in my gut like a kick. I desperately needed a break from the chaos. I needed a change of scenery. I called my sister, Lori, who lived four hours south of us, and asked if I could come and stay with her for a few days, or possibly a few weeks. I wanted to be around someone who loved me and could help me with my life. I was unwilling to get my children — or especially my parents — involved due to the extremely sensitive nature of the situation. The shame, helplessness, and hopelessness were consuming me.

After speaking to my sister a couple of times over a period of two days, she agreed to let me come and stay with her and her husband of almost 20 years. She could hear that I was desperate, but without knowing any of the facts, I believe she was mostly confused.

I called Paul at the state police post and told him that I needed to get out of the house. I said I was going to stay with my sister for a short time. "If you go, don't bother coming back," he said to me. "So, you're telling me that I can't go?" I asked. He laughed and said, "No. I'm telling you that if you go, don't bother coming back."

I was crushed at his lack of concern, but not surprised. Then I had an idea — I called my psychiatrist to ask him if there was a place where I could go to get help. I told him that it was important for me to go somewhere out of town and away from Paul. He immediately made arrangements for me to check into a psychiatric hospital located two hours south of our house. He said they were expecting me the very next morning and were holding a bed for me.

I called Paul again at the post and told him about the arrangements I had made with my doctor. He was fine with that scenario. He did not ask me why I wanted to go or the reasoning behind my request, but he did make it very clear that he had no problems with me going to a hospital. However, under no circumstances was he willing to "let" me stay with anyone in my family. My family, obviously, was a threat to him. What he wanted, what he had achieved was complete seclusion from anyone or anything outside of him and our home. That is why I was shocked when, the night before I was to check into the hospital, he gave me a $20.00 bill and said, "Here's some money for gas. Good luck." I was absolutely certain that he would drive me to the hospital and drop me off because that would put him in the position of control as per usual. But no. He left for work early the next morning without saying goodbye and I got up and drove myself down to the hospital. I called him on my way to let him know that I would not be contacting him while I was there. His response was simply, "Okay."

It was an exceptionally long, two-hour drive. By the time I arrived at my destination I was in full panic mode and crying uncontrollably. Of course, I had already known — for a very long time — that he did not care about me or even like me very much, but that did not deter my wish that he could or would love me in a true, real, normal way somehow or someday. I had never let go of my wish that he could be my knight in shining armor, a fantasy that I held onto tightly in the depth of my heart and soul. I really did love him immensely. I was in love with the man I wanted and never stopped expecting him to be.

At the hospital, I was checked in by a nurse who asked me several questions about my current state of mind and, for the first time ever, I was able to say the words "control" and "abuse" out loud. I told her that the abuse was at the hands of my own husband, who happened to be a police officer, but that was all. I was not able to discuss any details. The words were still unavailable to me. I still had not been able to convince my heart and soul of the true nature of the abuse, or even, really, admit to myself that it was abuse. I knew in my very being that once I accepted the fact that I was being abused, my life would change forever in a way unfathomable and unknowable. This was not a step I was willing to take. Not for many more months to come.

I will never be able to understand why I did not recognize these clear, concise, and blatantly obvious huge, neon signs of abuse. I was so blinded by him and my own hopes, my wishes, and my naiveté. I refused to see what was right in front of me. I can only tell the story of how it happened. I have long since learned to accept my stupidity and blindness and own up to my part in what happened. As I have mentioned, however, a storm was building inside of me. Before too long it would be unleashed to change everything in my life.

I remained at that hospital for over two weeks and was counselled by many mental health professionals. Several things were made clear to me during my stay, the most important of which was that if I did not get out and stay out of this relationship, I would end up dead. I was given a diagnosis of PTSD (post-traumatic stress disorder) and was urged not to return to my husband upon my release. They told me, in no uncertain terms, that he would eventually kill me, that all of the signs were screaming loudly. I had not revealed the horrid details about the extent of his abuse, but what I had discussed was obviously enough for them to warn me that my life was in danger.

I met several nice people during my stay, all of whom were patients. I will never forget one woman I spoke to while we were in classes together, and what she said to me. We were sharing with each other about our families and our troubles, and she said she had grown up and gone to high school in a small town on the west side of the state. When she mentioned the name of that small town, my mouth dropped open. That was the town where Paul had grown up! I told her my last name and, after confirming the names of Paul's older brothers and his parents, my friend became profoundly serious. She told me that she had dated one of his brothers in high school for a short time, and then she made a strange comment about his family being well known in that area, but "not in a good way." She took my hand and looked in my eyes and said, "You go home and get your things out of your house and run as fast as you can. Do not look back and keep running until you are miles and miles away, five states away is not even enough." I was shocked. I did not know what to think. Our group ended right then, and I could not wait until the next day, so I could speak with her again. But I never saw her. Another patient said she had left the hospital. I did not know her name or anything much about her. It was a strange encounter in every way.

When I returned home, I shared this story with many of my family members, all of whom were just as curious as I was about the story. I never did find out what it meant, although I hope to someday. I did find out, however, many years after my hospital stay, that one of the doctors who treated me called Paul at his post to discuss my fragile condition. She told him that I was suicidal and that I had said that I wanted to use his service weapon to kill myself. The doctor felt it was important for Paul to know this, and she tried to get him to agree to stop taking his weapon home in order to keep it away from me. Paul never mentioned this call. And he never stopped bringing his loaded gun home.

# CHAPTER 15: GET OUT, GET AWAY, DO IT SOON

After being released from the hospital, I went straight to my parents' house to seek solace and advice. Both of them were so supportive and loving, but I felt strongly that they were incapable of helping me get away from him, for many reasons. They were getting older, for one, and their ability to grasp all of the details would have been impossible — their naiveté was even greater than mine. They did, however, know that the situation was very unstable, unpredictable, possibly explosive. They shared their concerns that I should stay as far away as possible. They believed that Paul could be extremely dangerous. They pleaded with me to get the authorities involved. But we decided that I would not be staying there with them. The thought of him showing up at their house to confront me for any reason was a threat we were not willing to take. I had a strong feeling of respect and did not want to get them involved in any way. Protecting them was my top priority. None of us really knew what to do.

I had not spoken to Paul in over two weeks, so I called him and told him that I was back in town. He was happy to hear from me and asked when I was coming home. I had decided that I was going to tell Paul about my fear of him and my questions about my own safety. I assumed that the timing of my questions was more than appropriate since I had just returned from the hospital. But treading very lightly and cautiously was important. My anxiety was consuming me. I had many ideas but no real plans. I decided to take it one minute at a time and stay hyper-aware of his moods and his actions. That was my plan, and it seemed to be the only option. One. Minute. At. A. Time. Silently.

I arrived home and he greeted me with a hug and a kiss. He seemed calm and quiet and went about his usual routine of staying in the bedroom, glued to the computer, and playing his guitar. He did not talk to me at all — not one question about my stay at the hospital. He seemed oddly disinterested, and I had the immediate sense that he had called to check on me more than once over the past two weeks — not to see how I was doing, but to make sure I was still there.

For about two weeks he remained calm and quiet but continued to take complete advantage of me as his sperm receptacle and was more than happy to continue with the urination issue. He was much quieter about demanding that I perform sexual acts to please him, though. It seemed like there was a huge gap between us, one that had never been there before, a vastly different kind of gap.

One night he brought out a device that I had never seen. It was a hard, plastic contraption that fit tightly over his penis and testicles and locked into place. He described it as some sort of chastity device and brought up a picture of it on a website. I knew that he was not trying to be celibate — he was still engaging in intercourse with me. I thought that, if anything, he liked wearing the device simply because it caused him pain. I tried to get him to help me understand the what and why, but he had no explanation and I did not want to push it. I did not really want to know what or why. I was so full of depression and wonderment about both of our lives and where we had ended up — too many answers to my questions was not something I was prepared for. I was numb and unfeeling, incapable of bringing forth any real anger or unhappiness about anything. I was just existing in my life, not living it at all.

At the end of May, an invitation came in the mail for his niece's wedding in Oklahoma. We both looked at it, and he immediately told me that we could not attend because his daughter had her state track meet that weekend — she was set to compete, and he was the assistant coach. That was that. I had no opinion about it at all. Not that my sentiments about it one way or another mattered. He decided everything. I decided nothing. A week or two went by, and I was absolutely shocked when he called me into the bedroom one evening to inform me that he had decided to send me to attend the wedding as "a representative of our family." He said that he had already made all of the arrangements with his sister and his mother in Oklahoma. He said that he had purchased my plane ticket. I would be going by myself, and all of the arrangements were done. He was not asking me if I wanted to go, he was telling me that I was going.

I was perplexed. He had never done anything like this before. He could tell by my reaction that I was completely unsure and in shock. "Hey," he said, "I'm trying to do something nice for a change, can't you just accept it?" I was hesitant, but I said, "Okay, if you want to send me away on a trip to see your family, I will go." He went through the arrangements with me and it was decided — I would be gone for a total of five days. He would drop me off at the airport and pick me up at the end of the trip. I was starting to get excited at the thought of being away from him, on my own for five days, even though setting it all up before asking me about it seemed very presumptive. I did not dwell on that thought long. He could not have done it any other way due to his controlling nature.

Still, I was uneasy. The trip did not exactly feel like he was doing something special for me. I could not hide my angst that there had to be a reason. There had to be something that he was gaining for himself by sending me away. What exactly, I did not know. For the past several weeks he had been a kinder person, not so sexually demanding or needy. I automatically thought that he was getting his needs met somewhere else, but I really had no way of knowing.

And, sadly enough, I did not really care. I continued to dislike him more and more — even to the point of detesting him. He was acting better towards me, but there was a definite, underlying air about it, one I did not recognize. It just felt evil. It felt wrong. But it was definitely there, some unknown feeling that would grow from a soft whisper to a loud scream.

My trip was coming in a matter of days, and I went through my closet to begin picking out clothes to pack. I had to dig deep because the weather in Oklahoma at the end of May was much different than the spring weather in Michigan. I would have to find some shorts and tank tops to take with me. It had been an exceptionally long time since I had bought any new clothes for myself. I found some acceptable casual items, although nothing to wear to the wedding. Shoes, also, were going to be a problem. I set out to discuss this with him.

In a normal relationship — and in all of my past relationships — I would have simply gone out to buy what I needed, either with my own money or with a credit card, without any questions or problems. But with Paul, treading lightly, asking with fear and trepidation for permission to spend any amount of money — especially on something he deemed unnecessary — was not something I looked forward to. I approached him like a scared child with my request and, as was expected, he insisted that I did not need a new dress at all. As usual, he pointed out that I had a closet full of clothes. This was true, but most of those clothes did not fit me any longer or were not appropriate for the occasion or the season. I marched him into our large closet and went through almost every item hanging in my section, insisting that he pick something out that he thought would be appropriate. He agreed to take me shopping the next day.

He did, in fact, take me shopping the very next day. He took me to Goodwill, where I found a dress that he approved of for exactly $6.98. Goodwill, as you may or may not know, is a second-hand shop where people drop off items they no longer want or need. Yes, this story is true. The dress was rather ugly, but it was presentable and fit me well. He asked me, then, about any shoes I had that would match it. When I told him that I had none, he spent another $17.00 on a pair. I still find this to be so extreme, even for him. Extreme in the way of being ridiculous and cheap. Was I really that spoiled in my previous life to find this so ridiculous and cheap? Should I check myself and realize that this behavior is normal and what most husbands would do? I cannot get myself to believe that to be true, but I will accept and acknowledge that I really was spoiled in my previous life. I feel perfectly fine with that truth.

I had started to ask him, in the weeks prior to my trip, if he was going to be sending me with any money in my wallet, but I was tiptoeing around the question very carefully so as not to set him off. Whenever I brought it up, he would shut me down almost immediately, saying, "Don't worry, you will have money." Okay, fine, I thought. My flight was leaving early Wednesday morning, and the night before I packed my things and got everything ready. I was feeling anxious, and the mood in our bedroom was rather — more than usual — uncomfortable as we were attempting to fall asleep. We were both quiet, so I decided to ask him again about the money. I said, "So, you are sending me with some money tomorrow, aren't you?" His response, with a heavy sigh, was, "Don't worry, you will have money." I pushed the issue further and said something about not feeling comfortable about travelling without a credit card in case of an emergency. He laughed quietly and said, "Nothing is going to happen. You are only travelling for a day." I put it to rest at that point. I could feel his discontent and annoyance with my questions. Never, ever, did Paul like to be told "no." And he did not ever like to be questioned, period.

It was a quiet, two-hour ride to the airport with no radio and few words spoken. When we arrived, he walked me inside, saying he would take me to check in. Just inside the door, he turned around to face me and got his wallet out of his pocket. He reached in and handed me two $20.00 bills, then returned his wallet to his pocket. I was stunned. I looked at him and said, "This is $40.00." "Yes," he responded, "and you don't need any more than that." I said back to him, "You're not even going to send me with a credit card in case something happens?" "Nope. Nothing is going to happen." We then walked up to the check-in counter where the clerk informed me that she needed $20.00 as a fee for my luggage. Paul looked at me — I was still in shock, holding my $40.00 — and said, "Wow, you're really going to have to budget your money now," indicating that I should hand over half of my "allowance." I recovered enough to say right back, "There is no way in hell I am using one of these twenty dollar bills to pay for my suitcase, so you had better get out your bank card. And while you are at it, you better pay for my return trip because I will be flat broke by then." The clerk stared at me in disbelief. Paul let out a quiet, uncomfortable laugh and handed her a credit card. WTF. WTF. What a complete bastard! He walked me to the gate, waved goodbye, turned, and left.

I was still in shock. I felt completely defeated and controlled again, still, by my abuser-husband. Unfortunately, if you can imagine, this story gets much worse over the next twelve hours. I boarded the plane in tears. I had not eaten anything at all that day, and food is not served on flights anymore without a hefty price. A meal was out of the question.

We landed in Chicago at O'Hare Airport where I had a four-hour layover. I found my gate and tried to settle my anxiety and rest. I had strict instructions to call him at this point in my trip, so I took out my phone and did just that. He was short with me and said that he had to go but that I was to call him again as soon as I arrived in Oklahoma. He did say, however, before our conversation ended, "Oh, I forgot to tell you that I put a check for $60.00 in your wallet. It's made out to my mother, so if you need any more cash just give it to her and ask her to take it to the bank for you."! I did not know whether to feel grateful for his "generosity" or stupid like a 12-year-old child.

I was tired and so hungry, so I set out to find a quiet place to sit and have something to eat. I got a small table at Chili's and ordered a chicken salad and a diet Pepsi. I ate, trying to look forward to the few days ahead. My meal ticket, with a small tip, came to $16.00. That left a whopping $24.00 to my name. I did not feel any better, but I returned to my gate to wait for my flight. And then, bam — everything fell apart. It had been raining for most of the day in Chicago, and the storm was getting worse, much worse. Each and every flight out of the entire airport was delayed, time and time again, over the next several hours until, at 10:30 that evening, my flight was cancelled altogether until the next morning. Here was the "emergency" situation I had worried about. It had actually happened. And yes, it was absolutely an emergency situation in my mind. I was stuck at O'Hare International Airport overnight, by myself, with no money, no credit card, no bank card, and no checkbook. I had no means to get myself another meal, a room at a hotel, nothing. I was consumed with so many feelings, and none of them good. I was livid with anger and resentment. I remember thinking to myself, "Here I am, a grown, 47-year-old woman on a trip by herself and absolutely unable to get a hotel room for the night. How did I get to this place in my life?"

I had so much anger for him in that moment that I did not know how to act. I sat on an empty bench, crying relentlessly, with people walking by, staring at me. An older gentleman came over and put his hand on my shoulder and asked if I was all right. I told him I was fine and thanked him as he walked away. After sitting on that bench for a long time, I decided that I would call Paul to see if he had any bright ideas. I knew what his suggestion would be, but I had to hear it for myself. As soon as he picked up the phone — and before I could even get the words out — he said, "I know, I already know. Your flight got cancelled." He explained that he had gotten an e-mail from the airline. When he allowed me to speak, I said, "You son of a bitch," and many other choice phrases. I began crying again and hung up on him.

Over the next three hours we had phone call after phone call, back and forth, and it came down to the fact that he was completely unmoved by my dilemma. He said he would not get me a room for the night and advised that I was "just going to have to sleep in the airport." I spent every single second of those three hours crying and walking back and forth from floor to floor and terminal to terminal feeling completely out of control. I took the automatic people mover, which is like a big, flat escalator that moves you along without having to walk, probably 50 different times, back and forth. Everyone else in the airport was walking around in the same predicament, but I was certain that no one else in that entire facility was in the same, awful place that I was, financially and emotionally. What a son of a bitch. It was not even the fact that I had to sleep in the airport — which I could have done with no problem — it was the totality of the whole situation that angered me. I was deeply hurt.

Finally, after realizing how much time had passed and how late it was, I sat down to rest my aching body. I decided that I needed to come up with a plan. I had heard people talking about "taking a shuttle to a hotel," so I got up and waited in a long line to inquire about where I needed to go to get on one. The woman at the desk handed me a hotel voucher for 20% off. I took that and headed down to the street level where the shuttles ran. It was so nice to be outside that I simply sat down on the window ledge and watched and waited. Many people were waiting, and there were many shuttles from many different hotels. I could hear other people talking about all of them being filled up due to the storm. Then, word hit about a group of hotels outside of the airport area that still had rooms available. I decided to get on one of those shuttles with a group of other people. I was not sure what I was going to do when I got there, but at least I would be able to hang out in the lobby. I was so tired and so hungry, and my entire body felt like it was on fire.

After a 40-minute ride, we arrived at the hotel. In the lobby, there were so many people waiting to approach the counter that I decided to take a seat on the floor and wait until everyone had cleared out. I waited for over an hour. During the wait, I had decided to take my driver's license out of my wallet, along with a Michigan State Police I.D. card that had Paul's name, photo, and rank as sergeant. I took these two pieces of identification up to the counter and told the clerk my dilemma. I handed him my license explaining, "This is me." Then I handed him Paul's card, saying, "This is my husband." Then I burst into tears. I told the clerk, very emphatically, that my husband was an extremely controlling bastard and that he had sent me on a five-day trip with only $40.00 and no credit card or bank card. I asked him if he would be willing to call my husband to get his credit card number so that I could have a room for the night. The clerk became very serious. In a soft voice, he advised me that he would have to check with his supervisor because of the odd nature of my request. He was genuinely nice. He asked me to have a seat and said that he would be right back. When he returned to the desk, he said, "Yes, I will call your husband. Do you want to speak with him, or do you want me to handle it?" I told him that I did not want to speak to my husband at all and recited the number as he wrote it down. He dialed the phone, explained who he was and why he was calling, then said, "Do you want to give me your credit card number so that your wife can have a room for the night?" And that was that. It was done.

I took a hot bath, drank a diet Pepsi, and went to bed with the television on, wearing the same clothes I had put on that morning. I was a complete wreck and my mind was turning upside down. That unknown feeling that I had gotten weeks before, after I had returned from the hospital, felt like barbed wire in my stomach. I did not sleep at all that night. In the morning, I got up, rode the shuttle back to the airport, and got on my flight to Oklahoma.

* *

All in all, I had a good time with his family and the wedding was nice. I had a lot of fun with no pressure and no unreasonable rules. I stayed at his parent's house — as we always did when we travelled there to visit. I told Paul's mother about the check I had in her name, and she said that that she knew all about it, that Paul had discussed it with her. We went to the bank and she gave me the $60.00.

This entire money situation was so odd. And the fact that he had "discussed it" with her prior to my arrival gave me a very uneasy, creepy feeling. Does this seem weird and unbelievable, or is it just me?

At the end of my stay, one of Paul's family members dropped me off at the airport and I boarded my flight. It was the same route home, so I was due for another layover in Chicago. Wouldn't you know it? We sat on the tarmac in Tulsa for over three hours because the weather in Chicago was, once again, stormy, and rainy, just as it had been five days earlier. After sitting in that hot, sweaty, stagnant plane for all of that time, we finally took off and proceeded to Chicago. Once in Chicago, I ran to check where I needed to be to catch my flight home. Next to my gate number it said, "boarding." I was, of course, at one end of one terminal and the gate I needed was at the opposite end of a completely different terminal. I was in a panic. I ran as fast as I could, but somewhere along the run I slowed enough to check the flight status on the board again. Its status had changed from "boarding" to "departed." WTF.

I sat down to gather my breath and my thoughts, and the tears began to flow. I was so over it. I could not dwell on it for another minute or another day. The entire trip and all of its failures became like a blinding, neon sign that would not stop flashing. And that unknown feeling that had been planted in my stomach, that feeling which began as a soft whisper and got continually louder, was now the only sound I heard. It was screaming and ringing in my ears, "Get out, get away, do it soon!" The truth was showing itself to me as never before. Each and every act of abuse, control and manipulation over more than ten years was playing over and over like a slideshow in my mind. Like the click, click those old machines make when they flash a still photo on a white screen. One by one, on to the next — click, click. None of those still photos were like the ones I remembered seeing as a child. They were not the ones of me, my siblings, and my cousins gathered for a Sunday afternoon dinner at my Uncle Jake and Aunt Lois' farmhouse. They weren't the ones where we made ice cream in the old, ceramic crock with the hand-crank. We would all take turns, making sure the crock was surrounded by enough ice to make the cream freeze. Then, after we all had our big bowls of vanilla goodness, we would sit around on the floor, giggling and being silly while Uncle Jake proudly showed off his slides — all of us together on picnics and at the beach, smiling and laughing and simply being kids. Innocent little kids with dirty faces and wet bathing suits, barefoot and happy as clams, spending time together as family. No, not at all. These still photos playing over and over in my mind like a slideshow were scary and evil and sick. I was being raped and controlled. I was being made to do horrific acts. I was berated, manipulated, used, and abused. When was it going to end? It had to end.

In the meantime, my flight was gone, and I was stuck at the airport. Again. This time, however, I did not bother to call him. I proceeded straight to the street level to catch a shuttle to a hotel. I was much calmer this time. I was hell-bent to do whatever was necessary to get myself a room for the night. My anxiety was inexplicably non-existent. After a short time, a shuttle pulled up from the same exact hotel that I had stayed in five days earlier. I got right on.

Another 40-minute ride and we pulled up. I went inside with the few other passengers and, again, waited for the lobby to clear out. As I approached the counter, I saw him — the same clerk who had so kindly helped me out before. I smiled and said, "Do you remember me from last week?" He said that yes, he certainly did. I told him that I had missed my flight and asked about getting another room. He said, "Of course, ma'am. I think I still have your husband's credit card information right here." He turned around and looked through a stack of papers, pulled it right out and, turning back around to face me, said, "I will put this right through, and you'll be in your room in no time." That was that. It was done.

I got settled in my room and dialed Paul's number to let him know my whereabouts, but he, of course, already knew that I had missed my flight. He had gotten another e-mail from the airline when I rebooked a different flight for the next morning. We had a brief conversation, and he said he would be at the airport to pick me up. At this point I was, again, very tired, and very hungry. I had a total of four dollars in my wallet. I had paid for a couple of my own meals while in Oklahoma, and had also bought myself a fifth of alcohol one night when I rode to the liquor store with two of his brothers — something that I enjoyed during my time away, thank you very much.

Being back in a hotel room in Chicago was okay, too, since I took advantage of the last few hours that I would be free of Paul and all of his control and demands. I spent all four of my last dollars at the vending machine and did get a couple of hours sleep.

Early the next morning, I was back to the airport to catch my flight. I was on my way back home. The night before, I had laughed when I was walking around the airport because I wore my Detroit Red Wings spring jacket. It was white and had the big, red logo on the back. I did not wear it often, but it was the perfect coat to travel in and I really liked it. The irony was that a couple of nights prior, the Red Wings had just beat the Blackhawks to win the Stanley Cup. And here I was in Blackhawks territory, alone, with my Red Wings jacket and wearing it proudly. I thought that if I had to spend the night in the airport, I could have invited trouble. But we shall never know. Had I made the choice to do just that, my life might have turned out differently. I have thought of so many different scenarios and choices — both good and bad — but thoughts and fantasies of what might have been are a waste of good brain power. Off to my own reality, I was a few hours away from a life that was not really living.

There he was, waiting for me at the gate. Then, with a few short words about his family and the wedding, we were back at home. He did share with me, however, that he and his daughter had spent two nights in a motel while at the track meet. He told me that he and the other parents had planned to stay for two nights, and that he had also made plans for dinners out and other activities with their children. My suspicions of him gaining something from sending me away returned. Not only had he, most likely, spent hundreds of dollars on his little getaway, but I could not help feeling that something nefarious had occurred. He said that he had let his daughter stay with some of her friends in a separate room, leaving him alone for both nights in his. Nothing about this story makes any sense to me. I have held on to my suspicions, but I will never know the truth about any of it.

# CHAPTER 16: THE FIRE IS STOKED

Since returning from my trip, things between us were tense and uncomfortable, more so than usual. His sexual demands and ideas were increasing once again, and he brought forward some very unusual and creepy fantasies. He had stopped wearing the plastic "chastity" device because it was so tight that it gave him bruises, but he informed me that he had ordered another in a larger size. Then, he wanted to build a small "room" downstairs, some type of dungeon or torture chamber for me to "keep" him in. The "room" was an empty spot directly beneath the staircase, about ten feet long and three or four feet wide. I do not know the details of his plan, but I know part of it consisted of chains, handcuffs, and leg irons. There would be locks on the door too, so he could not get out. Just listening to his sadistic fantasies made me sick. I did not know how to respond to him anymore.

One night, when we were in the kitchen and he was sitting at the counter with his dog collar around his neck, he described another fantasy that he wanted me involved in. He said he wanted to masturbate on a plate of food that would be his dinner, and then he wanted me to set it on the floor. I would lead him over to the plate on his hands and knees, wearing his collar and the leash, so that he could then eat the plate of food like a dog, licking the plate clean. I was horrified and sickened when he explained this to me. I get the same awful feelings as I recall the incident to write it down. At the time, I had no words to speak. I began crying and asked him why he would ever want to do such a thing. I told him that I did not understand him. I said I refused to be involved in any way with such a demeaning, disgusting act. What would be next? How was I going to handle this? More importantly, *why* did I have to handle this? I felt like I could not breathe. What would he demand next? What was he capable of? That was a thought that scared me more than anything.

I will never forget an odd thing that happened on a weekday night, sometime in the last few weeks of this story. It was something that my daughter and I still discuss to this day because it was so odd and inexplicable.

We were all sitting around in the kitchen–living room area, watching television — myself, my daughter, and Paul's youngest daughter. Paul was sitting on one of the bar stools in the kitchen playing his guitar. He rarely played anywhere other than in the bedroom, so this fact alone was weird. All of us girls kept insisting he go to the bedroom to play because it was disruptive, and we could not hear the television.

Suddenly the doorbell rang, and although his daughter and I both jumped up, he jumped up even quicker saying, "I'll get it." We complied with his request and he went to the door and opened it. As soon as he opened the door, he turned around, walked back to his seat, and began playing his guitar. Meanwhile, a man entered the house. He closed the door behind him, took several steps into the living room, then just stood there.

This man was a complete stranger to me. No one else recognized him, either. The man just stood there and said nothing. Nobody said anything. Paul had opened the door and let this man into our house without speaking to him. The girls and I were shocked — we looked at each other, back and forth, then at this strange man. We were all speechless. Then we looked at Paul, as the man of the house, as if to say, "Who is this guy and why is he just standing there? Do something." Paul never spoke a word, never moved. He just continued playing his guitar. It was the strangest thing, and the silence was eerie. It was like we were all frozen in time. It was an extremely uncomfortable feeling. Several minutes passed, then the man simply turned around and went back out the door. How strange, how weird.

As soon as the door shut behind him, the three of us girls all began saying things like, "Who the hell was that?" "What just happened?" "Did you know that man?" Paul just laughed out loud, saying he did not know who he was and not to worry about it. I was very confused. I asked him why he did not confront the man. Why had he not asked him any questions about what he wanted or why he was he there? Paul had no response to my inquiries.

Later, after we had gone to bed, I asked him again about the strange incident. I almost accused him of knowing exactly who the stranger was, because it seemed as if he had expected him to show up. He denied that accusation. But it did feel like he knew the man. And it felt like he knew exactly why the man showed up. It was so odd and unusual, and my daughter agrees with me. Don't you think that a man would be much more protective of his family and his home? Doesn't it make sense that the man of the house would be more inquisitive of a stranger at the door and not let him wander into the house? Don't you think the man of the house would question a strange man in his house about who he was, what he wanted, and why he was here? Even the normal "Hi, can I help you with something?" would have been appropriate. Then, when you consider that the man of the house is a police officer as well — well, something was off about this entire incident. Scarily so. Protect and serve, right? A very strange occurrence for sure.

I do not have answers to so many of my questions but, as usual, I probably do not want to know.

I suddenly had a whole new dimension of fear — mostly for myself, but partly for him as well. He seemed to be slipping into some sort of deep, dark, evil pit. Somewhere that I wanted no part of. He had already taken me farther down into that deep, dark, evil pit than I had ever wanted to go — he took me unwillingly, forcefully. But that day I refused to concede. I refused to let it swallow me up. I would not give in. I would hold on tightly to my core values. I was bigger than the evil, sexual beast that seemed to be consuming him and possessing his very being.

But he was all in. He did not seem to care about the possible consequences or collateral damage. He was willing to eat from a plate drenched in his own sperm on the floor like an animal. He was inviting strange men into our home. He was willing to be locked in a small, dark room, chained up, excited in some odd and evil way. I did not understand it back then, and I do not understand today, all of these years later. I do know that I was more and more fearful every day. Fearful of him and what he might decide to do to me. Would he kill me, as he had threatened? What would he require of me sexually? This was some weird shit. And, like I have said time and time again, no, I am not making this stuff up. I could not make it up even if I tried. All of this was completely outside the realm of my imagining.

It all came to the surface of my soul one afternoon when he came home and presented me with a collar. Yes, a dog collar, for me to wear. He had always said that he wanted me to have one, but I wanted no part of it. He insisted that I at least try it on. Then, I used that little, two-letter word that he did not like to hear. I said, "No. I am not putting that thing around my neck and you cannot make me." I told him that I was not a dog and I was not wearing a collar for him, ever.

I cannot explain to you what this request did to me as a person, a wife, a woman. He was pushing me under in the cesspool. He was holding my head down, not letting me catch a breath. It did so much damage to my mind and to my heart. I felt totally disrespected and lowly. Again. This request, this blow, felt like a heavy log, a heavy log that is put on top of the pile of logs already there. It was the log that brings the entire pile crashing down because it just cannot take it anymore. Too many logs, too much abuse. The last log was too heavy. The last act of abuse too great.

Suddenly, the culmination of each and every act of abuse, control, and manipulation was brought up to the surface, as if this request to wear a dog collar had been a sharp spade viciously driven into the soil of my soul. It lifted and turned each and every violation out of its rooted hiding place. I was inundated with pain, disgust, and the shameful realization of the damage he had done to my body, my mind, my heart, and my soul. I ached inside with rotting poison as all of this torture and pain lay exposed. All of the deeply buried evil, with its deep roots, had wound itself around the good things in my life. Everything was rotting inside of me — the good and the bad, the positive and the negative. My feelings, thoughts, and emotions were suffocated, choked out, leaving emptiness and a deep, dark hole. I felt all but dead. Only my breath and my heartbeat were left to take.

Then, an unfamiliar fire started within me. It burned away all of the torture and pain that lay exposed. It was a fire that brought strength and reckoning to render my life clean and pure. I would somehow be new and reinvented, as a person and a woman.

Fire is a relentless and destructive force, erasing everything in its path and reducing it to ashes. But fire can also be controlled. It can be used in a positive manner to erase what is invasive, aggressive, and intrusive. It can bring renewal, promoting healthy regrowth and positive change. I did not know it then, but that fire was the beginning of a never-ending, protective burn that would prevent any more hurt or pain. It would also give me the strength to make some hard, final, chaos-ending decisions. It would bring my life full-circle, to a place not only different geographically but, more importantly, a different place emotionally and mentally. This was a place of preservation and safety for my body and mind. I knew I could not endure any more of his torture, and I was fearful of my reaction if things did not change.

There was really no hope for that. Even less without a solid plan. I was stuck.

There was a new, specific tension and eerie feeling in the air between us — almost as if we were engaged in a silent war. I was so afraid of him, in every sense, and I am certain he was disgusted with my denial of his new demands and my refusal to concede to his wishes. With things so volatile in the house, I was having trouble sleeping at night. I remember lying in our bed next to him, feeling uncomfortable about getting too close or touching him in any way. He seemed to have this evil aura coming off of his body — an aura that felt wrong and negative and poisonous. The bad vibes he emitted would almost push me out of bed they felt so strong and awful. I did not want to be next to him. He was scaring me with his body, his words, his eye contact, his demands, and his mere presence.

Then, it happened. His last act of blatant, horrific, violent, torturous abuse. It was the last time he would rape me or use me as his sperm receptacle. The last time. I decided this after he raped me anally, with force and contempt in every thrust. No care taken while I lay face down on our bed, hanging on tightly to the sheets and crying quietly as he verbalized his anger, his pleasure, his complete satisfaction upon completion of his horror. This time, things were different. This time, the word describing how he treated me and how he made me feel screamed clearly and loudly in my soul. The word "whore." He treated me like a whore. I certainly felt like a used, abused, taken-for-granted whore. And I was not a whore. I had never thought of myself as a whore. I would never be a whore. But somehow, I had let him make me feel like a whore, for years, without realizing it.

The fire was stoked now, and the flames would cause complete destruction. With those flames burning hot and out of control, I made the decision that he would never touch me again. His hands would never be put anywhere on my body ever again. He was done "talking at me" and he was done disrespecting me. I had had enough. It was over.

# CHAPTER 17: THE FIRE IS BURNING HOT

And it was over, just two days after his last violent act. Over for him because he lay bleeding and dead in our bed. Over for me because I had put three bullets in his body from his very own gun. It was the same gun that he so proudly said was ready to go, "just point and shoot." Indeed, it had worked exactly like he promised. I pointed it at him as he lay asleep and I shot him.

Obviously, I knew better than to ever even think about taking a life — but that was before. Before him. Before he so blatantly and purposefully decided to use me, control me, dominate me, demean me, target me, intimidate me, shame me, guilt me, belittle me, isolate me, manipulate me, diminish me, disrespect me, degrade me, stalk me, rape me, scar and bruise me as a person, make me live in fear and insist I become a whore and feel like a whore.

Worthless and insignificant I was not. Arrested and charged with first degree, open murder I was.

I knew all too well that that was exactly what would happen, but I was ready to face it. Just as he had so blatantly and purposefully wrecked me, I had blatantly and purposefully killed him to put an end to it. I shot him three times while he lay sleeping in our bed, and the instant it was done I felt a rush of electricity run up through my body from the bottom of my feet to the top of my head. It almost felt as though I had been cleansed inside. I left the bedroom and went out to the kitchen to call 911 to confess to what I had just done.

And so, my life changed. Completely. Although I have finally revealed the true tragedy of this story that ends with the taking of my husband's life, this is not the end of my journey in any way. Due to the unbelievable and astonishing blessings that occurred during the next year — and even beyond that time — I was not free in the literal sense, but figuratively, I was freer than I had been in over a decade. I had my life intact.

My decision to end his life to regain my own would come with many consequences, as expected. The first being my son, Chad, who was upstairs asleep in our house on the night I killed my husband. He did not hear the shots I fired, but he did hear me shout for him from the bottom of the stairs immediately following my actions. That was my first dose of real consequences, and I was numb and helpless as I watched him run down the stairs in utter disbelief at the words coming out of my mouth — "He's dead. I just killed him. He's dead."

I cannot speak of the absolute horror he must have felt looking at his own mother and hearing her confess to such a horrific act. He would leave the house at the direction of the 911 operator shortly following his descent down the stairs. He would begin his own path of coming to terms with the enormity of the tragic situation and I would not see him again for three months. The ties that bound us as mother and son could have so easily been completely severed if not for his unconditional love and understanding. God's work would become front and center, as well as never-ending and all-healing.

I stayed on the phone at the direction of the 911 operator, then proceeded to the front porch with my hands in the air when I saw the lights and heard the sirens coming up the driveway. I was immediately handcuffed and asked about the location of the gun by the deputy detective. I told him that I had placed it on the kitchen counter. His next question was, "What happened here tonight?" My response was, "He is a controlling, manipulative, son of a bitch." I was placed in the back of his police car and sat there on the front lawn, just outside of our front door, as police officers from the county and the state arrived and entered the house one by one. I knew or recognized each one of them.

Sitting in the back seat of that police car, still in my own front yard, I had the overwhelming urge to take off my wedding band. I immediately did this with my hands in handcuffs behind my back. I removed it and held it in my right hand. It was an oddly comfortable feeling. I was no longer wed to my abuser. I felt free of him once and for all. He had never allowed me to be without my wedding ring, and one time, years earlier, when it fell off of my finger into the sink because of my excessive, sudden weight loss, he bought me an exact replica, in a smaller size, the very next day.

I was taken to the sheriff's department and escorted into a small, cold room where the detective asked me if I had any bruises or marks on my body that needed to be photographed. I responded, "No, he was way too smart to leave any marks." He read me my Miranda Rights, then asked me if I wanted to make any statements or answer any questions. Or did I want an attorney? I advised him that I would not be saying anything, but, "I definitely need an attorney, don't you think?" He had been holding onto a yellow legal pad of paper which was now sitting on the desk. I reached over and placed my wedding ring on top of the legal pad and told him, "Here, you can take this. I cannot stand to have it."

# PART 2

# CHAPTER 1: AUGUST 10, 2009

After I turned in my wedding band, the detective escorted me to the front of the building where a female corrections officer booked me, took my picture, and directed me to take a shower, handing me a change of clothes. She actually took my picture after I got out of the shower, because my arrest photo shows me with slicked back, wet hair, looking every bit like a worn down, torn down, abused woman who had just committed murder. I felt much worse than I looked. I knew that whatever was going to happen to me would be, without a doubt, completely different than anything I could possibly imagine.

I was so scared of what was about to occur in my life, but I knew that I would somehow survive. I would make it through all that was about to happen. I knew I had God on my side — He had allowed me to live and breathe through a living hell; He would carry me to where He wanted me to be.

I sat in that office with the woman who was booking me in, and suddenly I had the overwhelming feeling that Paul was going to walk through the door. I was shocked at my actions, but I was also having an awfully hard time believing it was true. I remember saying to the officer, "Is this some kind of a joke? Is he really dead? Is he going to walk through that door to confront me?" Even as I said the words, I could smell the odor of the burnt gun powder in my nose. She assured me that it definitely was not a joke, that he was indeed deceased.

I was then placed in a room by myself. There was a wooden bench, surrounded by windows and in plain view of the officers outside. I lay on that hard wooden bench and cried on and off for what seemed like hours. These were the first few hours of being locked away. There would be many, many more to come.

Eventually, they moved me into the women's section of the small, county jail. They gave me a blanket and assigned me a bunk. I had not been given a pillow of any kind, and during my entire time in the county jail a pillow was not allowed. There were about six or seven other women there, and all of them were sleeping because it was early in the morning, this morning of August 10, 2009. It was just after midnight on this same day that I had shot and killed my husband-abuser.

*Why? Why did you kill him?* That was what everyone wanted to know — that was their very first question.

As I have mentioned many times, I had never told anyone explicitly about the abuse. I knew beyond a shadow of a doubt that I had killed him to save myself, but talking about the abuse, bringing it into the light, opening the door on that heavy box would be so much harder than I ever imagined. What had happened to me would take a long, long time to verbalize.

At first, the only thing I could say was that he was an asshole and he treated me awfully. That was it. That was all I could manage. Of course, it is much easier for me now, all of these years later, to recount the abuse in detail and write it down. But back then, it was utterly impossible. I had not really come to terms with the severe nature of it. I had not even taken that crucial first step of recognizing it as abuse or ever admitting it. It is so shameful. It is so hurtful to take it out, analyze it, and recognize it for exactly what it is — and then you have to accept it. Then, and only then, can you begin the healing process.

I have healed immensely in these past six years, but I will never be able to put it all behind me. It is who I am now. The experience shaped the woman I have become. I can take one step, and then another in this long, excruciating process. Overwhelming? Yes. Scary? Yes. Unknown? Absolutely. Possible and doable? I have no choice. I am ready to fight the good fight, yes.

# CHAPTER 2: FIRST DEGREE MURDER CHARGES

The next day was my arraignment. The judge would read the charges filed against me, take my initial plea, and set my bond, if any. I knew exactly how the court-side of things worked, but the unknown parts were, well, unknown. I did not sleep at all the first night in jail, and early in the morning I was surprised when a deputy came in to tell me, "Your attorney is here to see you."

My attorney? What attorney? Did I have an attorney? I knew many attorneys in the area from my days working at the courthouse and at law offices, but I had not contacted anyone — not even my family. In fact, I had decided that I would request a court-appointed attorney, at least until I could make some other arrangements. I knew that the entire tragic situation would be extremely hard for the people connected to me to fathom. I knew that what I had done would strip away a chunk of their hearts and change our relationships forever. And money is never an easy topic in a family circle. Asking for or expecting help to defend me on a murder charge was, shall I say, more than delicate. I had not even thought past taking his life and saving my own; I had not been able to fit anything else into my brain. A legal defense? I obviously knew I would need one, but I had not been able to think that far ahead.

So, there I was, being escorted to the jail library room to meet an unknown attorney, just a few short hours before I would face a judge. I walked in to find a tall, dark-haired man reaching out to shake my hand. He introduced himself as Jesse Williams — and I did know him! We had never met, but I had spoken to him on the phone once. He had called to speak with a woman attorney I was working for and, as she was out of the office, he left a message. He had been genuinely nice and chatty, and we had had a conversation about how he was looking for a legal secretary to work in his office. When I told him that I had worked in the field for 28 years, he jokingly asked me if I wanted to come to work for him. I laughed and said no, that I had a job, but I did know of someone currently searching for a job: my friend, Sandi. As it turned out, she got the job with him almost immediately and they were both happy.

Sandi also knew Paul quite well — she often would go to the post with me when I had to provide him with lunch, and the three of us would eat together and chat. She knew he was extremely controlling, but she looked at him as I did, as my family did, seeing the police officer persona first and foremost. That is what almost everyone saw when they met Paul. They gave him the benefit of the doubt by default because of his profession.

And it was Sandi who had urged Jesse Williams to the jail to see me on that early Monday morning. The news of Paul's death and its tragic nature had funneled down quickly from person to person, stunning Sandi beyond belief. According to Jesse, Sandi had been beside herself, crying all morning, and somehow, through the grief and disbelief she had inspired Jesse to offer to represent me on a pro bono basis in the interest of justice. I was shocked. I remember saying to him, "Do you have any idea how much work goes into a murder case?" Like I knew anything about it, which I really did not. But I could not help but feel that it would be time-consuming, draining, and expensive. Costs alone would be in the thousands of dollars. What I did know was how much attorneys charge by the hour, and what a statement for services rendered looked like. Every phone call, every letter sent and received, detailed in dollars. The fee for such a huge case was unimaginable.

But Jesse insisted he was not doing it for money — he was genuinely interested in the pursuit of justice. While Sandi did not specifically know about the abuse, she had been around us together as a couple, enough to be aware of his controlling nature, his awkward presence, and his extremely short leash on my activities. I am certain that when she was told that I had shot and killed him, all of her fears, doubts, and beliefs came together to confirm what she had already assumed.

I still, to this very day, do not know exactly what she said to Jesse to prompt him to take such a huge leap — but there he was, standing in front of me, offering his services in my time of need. We agreed that he would appear with me at the arraignment and enter his appearance on the record as my defense attorney. Still in shock from the entire event — all ten years of it — I did not think twice about his offer. I felt a sense of protection while with him, this man whom I had just met.

At the arraignment, the charges were read by the judge and I entered a plea of not guilty. The bond was denied outright. That had been assumed, and nothing could be done about the fact that I was automatically considered a threat to the community when charged with Open Murder. That the victim was a police officer no doubt made the bond consideration even more unlikely.

My entire family was at the arraignment, along with extended family and many friends. I was not allowed to speak to or get close to anyone sitting behind me in the gallery, but I was able to see the pain on their faces and the tears running from their eyes. The feelings of pain, remorse, and confusion were thick in the air. No one could believe what was happening. Much later in my journey, I would discover how my daughter and family members were informed of the tragedy, along with their broken-hearted reactions. I had seen with my own eyes the horrific reaction from my own son.

But I would have so many blessings given to me, the first of which was Jesse Williams and his unwavering desire to step up, believe in me, and believe in my case. The next amazing blessing came two or three days after my arraignment, and would prove to be the most amazing, unexpected godsend of all. Another attorney came forward, also willing to work towards the best outcome possible in the interest of justice. This attorney had been practicing law for over 50 years and at the time of my case, was 85-years old. I had met this awesome man a few times over the years and knew that he was one of the most respected attorneys in the state of Michigan. Dean Robb was a renowned civil rights hero and true fighter for equality, something of a celebrity. He had also represented other women in the state who had killed their abusive husbands. When the corrections officer informed me that Dean Robb was in the conference room, waiting to meet with me, I was speechless.

I found him in the small room, sitting with a smile on his face and an outstretched hand. He introduced himself and I looked at him in shock. "I know who you are, Mr. Robb," I said. Then I sat down in disbelief and astonishment and asked him the obvious question, "Why are *you* here?" He explained that he had been in the hospital for a minor procedure, and that he and his wife had watched the local news while resting in his hospital room. My arraignment brought many reporters and the local television stations to the courthouse for details about the wife who had killed her police officer-husband. We saw you on the television, he said, then told his wife, "that woman has been abused." He said that he saw the abuse by the look on my face and the way I carried myself. He continued by saying that he had already been in contact with Jesse Williams, and the two of them would work closely together. Jesse would be lead counsel, and Dean, with all of his experience and knowledge of the law in these particular defense cases, would advise. Together, they would work as hard as they could to defend me against the murder charges.

I was amazed by these two men's eagerness to take on this cause, particularly since neither of them, at that point, knew anything about me. They both had an innate sense of certainty that something awful had been going on — especially since I had taken such extreme measures to free myself. My case would last an entire year, and in that time these two special men would spend hours and hours with me, working tirelessly. There were other attorneys, too, who were equally moved to put their time and effort towards my defense.

For example, attorney Mike Swogger, a man I had known since high school, worked on Paul's probate case. The distribution of his pension, life insurance, and deferred compensation funds was completely separate from the criminal case. As his wife, I had been the main beneficiary of Paul's monetary benefits. But it is a well-known fact that if you kill your husband, and are convicted in a court of law, you automatically lose any and all rights to any benefits. I knew this was the case. But I did not kill my husband for monetary reasons — I took his life to save my own. I still had my breath, and no amount of money could ever pay for that. Mike appeared at all of the Probate Court hearings on Paul's estate, fighting the good fight for me in the name of abuse and domestic violence. In the end, and rightly so, his three children benefited equally from his estate.

Then, there was Jim Amberg, a young, aggressive attorney who was kind and compassionate towards me. I remember at my Preliminary Examination, Jim took the podium to question witnesses and argue for me. His eloquence and expressive nature in the courtroom were amazing to watch and exciting to listen to. He, too, is a great man.

The Preliminary Examination was when I found out where the three bullets landed in Paul's body when I shot him. It had been dark in the house that night, and I did not look at his body after the shooting. I refused to go back into the bedroom. I was afraid. I did not want to see him lying there, bleeding, and dead. I was not at all proud or high-and-mighty about what I had done. It will forever be the worst decision I have ever made in my life. But it will also be the most important decision. Sitting in the courtroom, listening to the medical examiner describe his wounds and the cause of his death was stomach-turning for me. I had feelings at each end of the spectrum about what I had done. To this very day, I am completely torn about how, exactly, I am supposed to feel. I cannot seem to get comfortable with either end of the feelings, swinging back and forth: *I did what I had to do to save myself — Justification // Oh my God, I took his life, how could I have done that? — Devastation.*

What I did decide early on was that I would refuse to look at myself as a victim or a murderer. I would live my life believing that I am a true survivor. The truth is that I am a victim, a murderer, and a survivor. No one can tell me or convince me not to accept and live out all of those titles. I believe that, over time, I will come to terms with them.

The medical examiner's revelation of where exactly the three bullets penetrated Paul's body was easy for me to explain to myself. The first one hit him in his chest and went to his heart. The second one hit him in the corner of his mouth. And the third one hit him at the base of his skull, in the back of his head. To me, those bullets were on target — his dark, deceitful heart; the demeaning words coming from his mouth; and the maniacal, sadistic thoughts buried deep in his mind.

*Justification* and *devastation.* Back and forth, it is a constant, emotional struggle that has caused high blood pressure, extreme anxiety, sleep deprivation, and an ongoing ulcer in my stomach. Is feeling justified right or wrong? Is feeling devastated right or wrong? This will forever be my dilemma and my rightful punishment. However, no one else but me has to carry this burden for the remainder of my life.

At the conclusion of the Preliminary Examination, my case was bound over from District Court to Circuit Court for purposes of a trial, as was expected.

# CHAPTER 3: OUT ON BOND

As you can imagine, I was not doing well emotionally or physically. Although I had consciously, with forethought, made the decision to end my husband's life — actually killing him and living with that decision was way more difficult than I could have ever tried to imagine. Not that I had ever truly imagined it, but I had carried out that decision, justified or not, and now I had to face the consequences.

Apart from the devastation I had caused his family and my own, the immediate consequences to my body and emotions were needing attention. I could barely concentrate on living minute to minute. I lay on my bunk, in the jail, in the fetal position, covered up under my blanket, breathing in my own stale air. I needed to hide myself from the world, and being under that blanket, in my own little cocoon made me feel invisible and untouchable. I needed time to look deep within myself, to assess the damage done not only by him, but by myself, through my own actions. The cocoon made me feel safe for the first time in years, and it would be my hang-out place for most of the next year.

Three months after my arrest, my physical health began showing serious signs of distress. I was having chest pains and trouble catching my breath. With a history of heart disease on my father's side of the family, it was a real concern for me and my attorneys. I was able to make an appointment to see my primary care doctor — the doctor I had been seeing for years — and was taken from the jail to my appointment in handcuffs, belly chains, and leg irons by corrections' officers. It was a difficult day and I cried most of the time, but the doctor was gentle, understanding, and caring. I have always loved and respected him, and his continuing support was heart-warming. He decided that I needed to have my heart checked out, and I was scheduled for a heart catheter procedure in a few days. Suddenly and very unexpectedly, I found myself sitting back in the courtroom between Jesse and Dean as they argued a motion for me to be granted a bond in order to address my health concerns. I was shocked, stunned, and very apprehensive about being bonded out of jail on a murder charge, but my counsel was confident. The motion was granted, with the agreement of the county prosecutor, and I was released to the custody of my parents with a tether on my ankle.

What a huge, unexpected blessing! I left the jail and went home — home to the house I grew up in and loved so dearly. It was mid-October 2009, and I took in every minute with my mom and dad, holding on tightly to cherished memories. Over Thanksgiving, Christmas, and New Year's Day, I was able to see my children, my friends, and many of my extended family members — it was more than I could have ever asked for. I was also able to spend a week in the hospital as a patient under the care of some mental health professionals, and the catheter procedure found my heart to be healthy and working well. Still, so much was happening all at once, and I was overwhelmed with emotion and the knowledge that my life was about to change in many different ways.

During this time with my parents, Dean Robb reached out to a local forensic psychologist who agreed, at his (Dean's) urging, to see me. So began a three-month period of talking and evaluation with Barbara Jones-Smith, a wonderful woman whose kindness and willingness to put forth her time and effort was yet another blessing from God. With her help, I was able to begin the revelation process.

I can only say that it was excruciating. One by one, she drew out the facts of trauma and abuse. Letting those details escape out into the open to be known by others made me feel dirty and worthless. I was so ashamed. The facts were so immoral. And the fear of being judged and questioned was terrifying. Truthfully, I was more prepared, more comfortable being judged and questioned about the act of murder than I was about the abuse and trauma. The act of killing him was something that I had decided to do on my own. It was a purposeful, intentional act made with a clear conscience — horrifically so — but my own decision, nonetheless. On the other hand, my husband's intentional trauma and abuse was never my decision, that was always out of my control, and I had pushed it down and buried it to root and rot.

In so many ways, the process was like revealing a big lie; like admitting something that you never wanted anyone to know about; like describing, out loud, something very bad that you had done and always wished you could take back. I was so ashamed, and the fact that the truth was not a lie and was definitely not something that I had chosen for myself, did not cushion that shameful feeling. I also knew that the truth would add yet another layer of pain, disbelief, and guilt to the lives of so many people. How were my children and family to come to terms with the truth, the awful truth of what had occurred in my relationship with Paul? At least they would have some answers and a reason for their concerns and questions. Although the answers do not make the reality of how I handled the situation any easier.

I also met with that forensic psychologist two times a week for a period of three months, and she administered multiple psychological and behavioral tests. I was happy when her final report concluded that I "was not considered to have psychopathological traits." Thank God, I am really not a psychopath. That did not mean that I do not suffer from other mental disorders, but the affirmation that I was not crazy or that far off the scope of normalcy was a huge relief. Being diagnosed with depression, anxiety, bipolar disorder, and PTSD is enough to live with on a daily basis; knowing that I am still intelligent enough to form whole sentences with proper language is a blessing.

After New Year's, the prosecuting attorney filed a motion with the court to revoke my bond, based on the fact that my health issues were cleared up. More importantly from their perspective, I was a threat to the community because I was a suspect in a murder case — they wanted me back in jail. I returned to the same bottom bunk in the county jail and the safety of my under-blanket cocoon. I felt so at peace there, all alone. No one could touch, use, or abuse me. I was thankful that God had sent an army of angels to be with me in that small corner of the world and I found solace in my invisibility.

# CHAPTER 4: TRUE EVIL

After my arrest there were investigations pending on behalf of both the prosecutor's office and my defense team, and many began at our house. Some of my family members, including my children and my two sisters, went to the house to retrieve personal belongings and small items that were meaningful to me. Both of my sisters' spouses accompanied them but refused to go inside. Everyone there on that day spoke of the evil aura that surrounded the house. Inside, in every room, it was even more present and palpable. My sister, Lori, told me that the air was thick, almost as if there were forces pushing and resisting in the environment. I am sure that some of these feelings were brought on by the circumstances of what had happened there, but I also believe that my children and my sisters — who are all Christians and hold Jesus close in their hearts — could feel the good and the bad, the positive and the negative warring with each other in the air. My sister told me that they prayed on the front porch before they went in, for extra protection.

Each one of them took items of mine for safe keeping, but all of the furniture and other household items were auctioned off as part of Paul's estate. The house itself was foreclosed on and sold at a minimal price, due to the fact that someone had been killed there.

My sister, Lori, took a small, two-tiered wooden plant stand to use in her house. Months later, during a conversation that we had on the phone, I was shocked at what she told me. She said that she had placed the plant stand in her living room and had lost at least six live, healthy plants after putting them on the stand. She could not figure out what was wrong. Lori has her license as a master gardener and a bachelor's degree in forestry. She has never killed a plant in her entire life, and she certainly knows how to bring sick, weary plants back to good health. She said that she thought she was losing her green thumb. But when I told her that that small plant stand had been one of the few items that Paul had brought into the relationship, it suddenly all made sense. Those plants were having the life sucked out of them by an evil, black force. This was my first thought, and she agreed with me entirely. She broke that stand into pieces and burned it in her fireplace.

I did not give this story another thought until one day I called my daughter on the phone. She said she was so glad to speak with me because she wanted to tell me about a radio she had taken that had started on fire, almost burning her house down. Paul and I had two or three radios that were in different rooms, and Ashley had taken one of them, a portable with really good speakers. It, too, had been Paul's. She said that one day it simply began shooting sparks and then burning with flames. When I told her about the plant stand killing the plants, we both agreed that evil spirits seemed to be present in items that had been his. How scary and how weird.

My good friend, Sandi, also spent time at the house, cleaning out the refrigerator and the cupboards and doing other tasks at Jesse Williams' request. Jesse went to the house as well, searching in every corner from top to bottom. He found some very interesting items during his searches, the most helpful being hundreds of images copied off of the computer and stored on discs. Jesse had had the idea of lying down on the bedroom floor to look up under Paul's desk, and there he found several of these disks taped to the bottom of the drawer. The disks contained hundreds of images of torture, of sadness, of evil, of people crying, of people being sodomized, poked, made to bleed, made to

164 | JONI ANKERSON

cry, made to hurt. Pornographic, sexual, violent images that Paul obsessed over and could not escape from. Jesse also found a box, delivered by UPS, sitting on the front porch. The box contained the new, larger-sized chastity device which Paul had ordered shortly before his death. There were other items found in the attic, but I have not been able to discuss with anyone what exactly those items were. There are many things that came to light about Paul and his activities during the investigations. Perhaps, someday, when I am able, I will learn more about these things.

My case was put on the trial docket for July of 2010 and, following the Preliminary Exam, the investigation kicked into high gear. Jesse retained the help of a computer forensics expert to analyze the computer, and he also received help from a private investigator to interview witnesses. That investigator, Michael Neihardt, worked many hours on my case, pro bono, and various facts came to light as a result of his work. For instance, a man who worked at the local Home Depot, had this story to tell:

> Statement prepared by Mr. Neihardt. "The witness explained that his contact with Melvin "Paul" Holbrook was about six years ago. For about a week, Paul Holbrook was coming into Home Depot looking to purchase floor covering. The witness and Paul had a lot of conversations about building materials, floor covering, etc. Paul came in wearing shorts and he had some type of brace on his knees. It was during those conversations that the witness learned that Paul was a State Trooper, and that he was off on leave because of injuries to his knee. Later in the week, Paul came into Home Depot with his wife, Joni. The witness explained that this incident stuck with him, and he remembered every detail concerning this. All of this information came back to him when there were news stories about Joni's

arrest. The witness commented that Joni stayed so far behind Paul, creating such a distance between the two of them, it was "almost like he led her on a leash." Joni stayed in the background during this entire time. The witness explained that during the time Paul was not making any decisions about floor covering, the witness was trying to engage Joni in conversations, the witness noted that Joni had a black eye and (what he described as) a broken nose. He said that the black eye was very obvious. Her nose appeared to be broken because he could see the twist and the wrinkles, therefore making it look like a broken nose. These things were very obvious. The conversation then began to continue concerning some floor covering; some item had been picked out. Joni was asked something about it, and she disagreed with the decision regarding the flooring. Paul Holbrook turned to Joni and screamed at her "You just shut the fuck up!" This incident has bothered the witness since it occurred. When he saw the news reports, he felt like he needed to come forward and explain what he saw." End of statement.

Mr. Neihardt was also able to interview Paul's first wife, Starr, who I mentioned earlier in this story. Starr was forthcoming and helpful in the defense of my case, and she would have surely been one of the most compelling witnesses in the trial. In an interview, Mr. Neihardt found out that Starr, too, had shot at Paul one night, with every intention of killing him. They had been having many problems, and Paul was engaged in multiple affairs with other women and lying to her about many things. Starr had loaded her gun and was waiting for him to come home. Just before he arrived, though, one of the children began fussing upstairs. Starr realized that if she killed Paul, someone else would be taking care of her children and she did not want that. She was mad, but instead of killing him, she walked outside when he drove in and shot in the ground next to his foot. When he got back in his car to leave, she shot again in the direction of his car. A state police sergeant called Starr that night, and later came to her house to speak to her in person. He commented to her about how they all understood the problems that Paul had been putting her through. Interestingly, no charges were filed, and the entire incident was simply swept under the rug. Starr did write a letter to the judge sitting on my case, and it is part of the court file at the county courthouse. These are her words: (in part)

"I feel that Joni and I have similar parallels in our lives with Paul. I felt the pain of which we both knew from Paul, emotional (sic), mentally, and physically. I took a shot at Paul towards the ground near him in my case to get his attention, he had pushed me to the breaking point. I needed answers as to how and why he could treat the one person he loved the way he was with the deception, hurt and lies that had taken place in our life. He never did answer that question, and now I will never get the closure I needed from him. I so understand why Joni felt there was no other way out of the situation she was in with Paul. I also felt that there was no way out from every controlling area of my life that Paul controlled. He controlled our money, where I could and could not go, to how much I had to weigh to the clothes I had to wear. He took call waiting off our phone (I did not know this) so when he was working, he knew when I was on the phone, he would then come home and want to know who I was talking to. He controlled what we did as a family which was always around his sports from softball in the summer to basketball in the fall and the winter. Our only family vacations were to his parents out of state. When we did visit my parents, I would have to go to the bathroom with him and sit till he was done and then I could leave. Our home had to be clean at all times also. Paul had had numerous affairs throughout our marriage, none of which I knew who they were with. The only one he told me about was with "AC." When he started seeing her, he made me go shopping with him for a new wardrobe for his dates with her. The pain in my heart that day I can still remember. At that point he moved out of our home, when he did this, he took my name off our bank account leaving me with no money. I was not working at the time. This was his way of controlling where I could go. He would pay our bills and take me grocery shopping. He came home one day and told the kids and I that he was moving us to my parents that weekend and I needed to start packing. I had to call my parents while he was there and tell them that the kids and I were moving back. Paul gave me everything in our home but our bed, he said he did this to show "AC" how much he was giving up for her. I got a job and moved out of their home and at that point I told him to stay away from us. I was at work one day and a neighbor called me and said Paul was climbing in my bedroom window. He always seemed to know where I was at. The kids and I went to a hotel for the weekend to just get away and he showed up there. How he found us I still do not know. The kids and I went to a friend's house for the weekend and Paul came in the night and took my car and left his car, this was done so I would know he was there and knew where I was at all times. I didn't know he had a key to my car. Shortly after that, "AC" ended the affair with Paul. He came to my home and told me it was over, and he wanted the kids and I back as a family. For whatever reason I moved the kids and I back to Coldwater with him. I was back a short time and women started calling. I finally got tired of it and asked one of the women what she wanted. She told me that she was seeing Paul. I told her I was his wife and she said no, he was divorced, he told her I was his cleaning lady. Shortly after, with the Grace of God, I found the strength to leave Paul and file for divorce. I moved out to the house and took my things with me. I was at my parent's house one weekend when the kids and I came home Paul had gotten into my home and moved everything, even the kids (sic) beds and dressers, to his house. I knew I had to leave the area to try and get away from him, which I did. Our divorce became final 6 months later, but it was a few years before he totally left me alone. Paul's relationship was good in the beginning of our divorce with our children (sic). When he started seeing other women my children never knew where or with who (sic) they would be spending their weekends with. They stopped going for weekends with their dad shortly after that. Our daughter tried to keep in touch and see her dad but that was short lived (sic). Our son had not seen or spoken to his dad since he graduated from high school, our son to this day does not understand why his dad just walked out of his life. Our daughter was married in 2008. She had been talking to her dad about it and he told her he, Joni and his youngest daughter would be at her wedding. They never came to her wedding. Do you know how hard it was to look my daughter in the eyes and tell her that her dad is not there? The hurt in her eyes was so painful to me. How could a dad do that to his daughter is unforgivable (sic). They never spoke after that. Paul was a strong and strange sexual being. With that said, I feel very uncomfortable talking about this, but it was who he was and how he abused and used control in his life. I will just name a few points and if you have any questions or need more information you can contact me. Paul was into bondage to the point of it being scary to me, to the point of it hurting me. He loved to dress in women's' (sic) underwear and enjoyed wearing it daily. He made me do his makeup and nails. He had many piercings that he did himself and I had to watch when he did this. His piercing did cause me pain when we had intercourse. I was told I had to do these things, or he would find someone who would, and I knew he would do that, so I did as I was told. When he wanted sex, I had to do as he said even if I did not want to or if our children were home it did not matter. He was in to (sic) pain. He enjoyed this very much. I hope you understand him a little better. Paul was good at being who or what he needed to be with different people and situations. At work he was a totally different person than at home. Like I stated my parents knew nothing of our problems. I was told by him that I could not talk to them about it. As for Joni, I have said I truly understand her feeling of being pushed to the point she felt her only way out was to kill Paul. I know how he would have stalked her had she left. I am saddened that she could not break free from his control. She took my children's dad, yes, their relationship was not exciting, but they held hope that someday he would reach out to them and that will never happen due to Joni's actions. Paul was a very evil man and hurt many people when he was on this earth, my thought is and what helps me to deal with this situation is he cannot hurt anyone ever again." End of letter from Starr.

I was in prison when I received the first letter from Starr. It was a beautiful card with a photograph of some delicate, lavender flowers on the front. The inside was blank, and Starr filled that blank space with kind words and the verification that she had experienced the very same sexual abuse, the same control, manipulation, and mental and emotional anguish at Paul's hands as I. She told me how sorry she was and made me feel almost justified in my own horrific actions.

Feeling justified in the intentional killing of a human being is beyond what is right and what is just. I certainly never imagined that I would put the words "murder" and "justification" into the same sentence and have it applied so directly to me and my life. Coming to terms with the fact that these two things were carried out by me, with a knowing and accepting conscience, is even more unbelievable and inconceivable. Going back and forth every day for the last six-plus years between feeling both justification and devastation for what I have done has caused great turmoil in my heart and soul. I do not know if I will ever resolve this constant stirring within me.

According to Webster, the definition of "justification" is as follows: *"1. a justifying or being justified; 2. a fact that justifies or vindicates; 3. the state or condition necessary for salvation, of being blameless or absolved of the guilt of sin."* The word "justify" as defined by Webster is: *"1. to show to be just, right, or in accord with reason; vindicate; 2. to supply good or lawful grounds for; to warrant; 3. to free from blame; declare guiltless; absolve."* The definition of the other, opposite feeling I experience on a daily basis, "devastation," is defined as: *"devastating or being devastated; destruction; desolation."* In kind, the word "devastate" is defined by Webster as: *"1. to lay waste; make desolate; ravage; destroy; 2. to make helpless; overwhelm."* As I look at each description, I feel that they both describe exactly where I find myself emotionally and mentally. But I also try to apply the words and meanings to Paul, and I feel that they fit into his side of the tragedy as well, but in an entirely different way. Paul felt *justification* in his deliberate infliction of *devastation* upon me and my body because of his extreme arrogance and narcissism, together with his inability to be empathetic, caring, or considerate in any way.

Starr and I corresponded back and forth about four different times while I was here in prison. I believe that someday the two of us will be able to sit down together to share our experiences and strength in our shared trauma. If that experience does not come to pass, I am comfortable with the kind words and conversations we were able to share through letters. It may be best to simply leave it at that, with both of us putting to rest our unfortunate marriages to the same deceitful, abusive man. It may be best to move forward with our lives without guilt or negative memories.

Michael Neihardt spent many hours investigating the facts of my case, and I will be forever indebted to him. I was able to obtain a copy of his Post-Conviction Confidential Memo, which is also a part of the court file. It states, verbatim, as follows:

> "It is my hope that you found the Holbrook investigation comprehensive and thorough. Based on witness interviews, client information and physical evidence, the Holbrook investigation was singular in terms of the extensive, extreme, and accelerating abuse that was involved in this relationship. Because of exclusive access to defense witnesses and client information, evidence was

gathered reflecting the extensive abuse suffered by Joni Holbrook. This abuse included her being required to view pornography showing physical abuse, such as a woman's vaginal (sic) being sewed shut, extreme physical abuse to obtain sexual gratification, demoralizing activities that reduced Joni Holbrook to the point where she could not see an avenue of escaping Paul Holbrook. The demoralizing activity included having to wear the same matching underwear as Paul Holbrook, the requirement to strap on a dildo and give Paul Holbrook anal sex for his gratification and playing the "rape game" so extensively that she was repeatedly raped by Paul Holbrook. Paul Holbrook lived every minute of his days thinking about sex and how to satisfy his sexual desires. Evidence was obtained which included pornography, restraints, and women's clothing; these items helped substantiate Joni Holbrook's abuse. It should also be noted that a retired State Police Officer who had had contact with Paul Holbrook many years ago made the statement (to the Michigan State Police) that if Paul Holbrook continued in his position, "someone would get hurt." Joni Holbrook found it impossible to leave Paul Holbrook and to obtain authoritative assistance because of her husband's position as a sergeant with the Michigan State Police. Several witnesses had asked if they could call the police; Joni repeatedly responded that she could not call the police because her husband was the police." End of Confidential Memo by Michael Neihardt, Investigator.

# CHAPTER 5:
# MANDATORY LIFE

My jury trial was scheduled to begin on July 14, 2010, and the weeks leading up to it were filled with anxiety. I spent most of the time locked in my protective cocoon, but even there I was becoming more and more apprehensive about my future. I was going on trial for Open-First Degree Murder, which carries a mandatory sentence of life in prison. That word, "mandatory," was beginning to haunt me.

I remember meeting with Jesse in this time before the trial and discussing the possible outcomes. When he reminded me of the mandatory life sentence — were I to be found guilty of the original charge — it was as though a building had suddenly fallen on top of me. Yes, I knew this was the law, but it was still crushing.

The word "mandatory" does not really stand out in normal, everyday terms, but when it is attached to "life in prison," it takes on an entirely new meaning. Webster defines this word, as *"authoritatively commanded or required; obligatory."* What this means is, that if and when I was found guilty by a jury of my peers, the judge would have no choice but to send me to prison for mandatory, required, obligatory life.

Now that I am here in prison, with all different kinds of women on all different kinds of charges, I have discovered that most of them have sentence terms in numbers like 10 to 20 years or 4 to 8 years. This means that they must serve at least the minimum term, but no more than the maximum term. Being sentenced to letters that spell "LIFE" is much different and causes emotions and feelings unimaginable to most of us. I have met many women here who have been sentenced to that fate.

When I made the decision to take Paul's life, I knew that I *could* spend the remainder of my life in prison. But at that moment I honestly believed I would be better off. I felt that I had no other choice — that it was the only way to keep him away from me. I knew the consequences and was ready to face the worst outcome because I *had* gotten away from him with my life. I knew I had it in me to fight the good fight, whatever that turned out to be. I also knew *for certain* that I had done the necessary, only thing to save myself.

But now, on the other side, the marriage over and Paul dead, I could not help looking at it from a completely different place. Yes, it was frightening, unimaginable, and unknowable, but for some reason it was also quietly and concretely comfortable. Feeling comfortable while facing a jury trial for murder and a possible life sentence in prison sounds strange, but somehow, facing this unknown felt more acceptable than the horrid life I had lived with Paul. The trial and its possible outcome seemed like the lesser of two evils in my life, and that thought brought an unfamiliar strength, perseverance, and resilience, fully replacing the negative and cynical feelings which had been injected into me by my abuser to root and rot. These positive, unfamiliar feelings were welcome and purposeful tools for me to use to overpower and heal. I felt as though I was winning my battle to become new again. I felt empowered to fight with this new strength and turn myself around to become the confident, worthy, fearless, bold, determined woman I knew I could be. Yes, it still seemed like a huge feat, but smaller in comparison to what I had already endured.

It was getting down to the wire, time was ticking away, and the reality of the jury trial loomed with its mid-week start on Wednesday, July 14, 2010. There had been much preparation on the side of the prosecution and tireless investigation and preparedness realized by my defense team. Several witnesses were subpoenaed to testify on both sides of the aisle.

Dean spoke to me many different times about his hopeful intentions to use the Battered Woman's Defense on my behalf. The criteria of the defense are astonishingly approximate to the terms and thresholds when applied to my case and its facts of abuse. The problem is that the Battered Woman's Defense is not recognized by the State of Michigan, even though many other states use it and apply it accordingly. Therefore, the defense could not be presented outright as such, and would have to be comingled, in my case, with a form of self-defense. I do not really understand it exactly, but I do know that without such an explicit defense like the Battered Woman's Defense, there are many women in the state of Michigan who have ended up in prison for life, after years of abuse and torture, because they killed their abusive husbands. These women were found guilty and convicted of a First Degree or Open Murder charge and sentenced to that fate because they were not afforded the benefits of an explicit defense law to apply to their own cases as is afforded other defendants in many other states. This is an outright injustice and robs these victims of the ability to fight and stand up for themselves. The women here in this prison for the same crime that I am guilty of are completely broken and helpless. Some here for life and some have been granted the possibility of parole, but only after serving at least 20 years.

I understand that each and every case is different and unique in its own right; however, each and every woman who endured horrific abuse and who took the life of their abuser to escape has, without question, lived in and experienced the same helplessness and fear that I did and should be entitled to use and apply the specific terms of a proper defense. I trust and believe that most of the women living life in prison for killing their abusers are good, honest mothers and daughters who found themselves in impossible, unimaginable, inescapable situations. I have come to this conclusion after making the excruciatingly difficult decision myself to take a life. I have to believe that, like me, their decisions only came at the point when enduring even one more minute of abuse was too much. I also believe that, at that very moment, when a woman decides she has had enough, she also plants a seed of strength, perseverance, and resilience — a seed that can make them whole again and able to endure whatever the consequences for their actions are.

Let us be realistic and admit that making the decision to take your abuser's life and breath is not that of a weak and wrecked woman. That decision, that action comes at the exact moment when your entire being says "no more." It is the moment when a woman decides to move forward and save her life. Women who have killed their abusers are not murderers, they are simply women who want to LIVE. Unfortunately, these women are placed on the same playing field as people who have killed for money, for drugs, for revenge, for gain — outright evil, criminally minded, uncaring people. Victims of horrific abuse are none of these. Their only consideration at the moment they commit the decided act is for the preservation for their own life.

For this reason, I will be one of the biggest, loudest advocates for victims of abuse when I am released from prison. I will attempt to move Michigan forward towards a clear and concise understanding of the traumatic effects such abuse has on women, women who act out in desperation to stay alive. These women have been through hell on earth at the hands of someone who claimed to love them, but instead used, controlled, dominated, demeaned, targeted, intimidated, shamed, guilted, belittled, isolated, manipulated, diminished, disrespected, raped, degraded, stalked, scarred, and bruised them. They lived in fear and terror. This experience brings them directly to the decision to kill, to stop the threat, to get out, period. No compassionate, caring, thoughtful woman would ever dream of committing murder without being pushed past the line of common sense.

At the same time, I do not believe that these women act spontaneously or impulsively and kill suddenly after one certain act of abuse. The murderous action is brewed and stirred and seasoned over years of purposeful abuse. The act occurs when appointed by their own body's definition of "enough," "no more," and "the time is now." It almost becomes an earned right by us victims, inasmuch as our abusers felt it was their earned right to purposely inflict the traumatic abuse. I realize this explanation is way out of the realm of acceptance for most people, yet, for me, it is the awful truth. Murder is not the first thought that comes to mind in an abusive situation, but eventually, it feels like the only option for survival.

# CHAPTER 6: INEXPLICABLE PREPARATION

On the Friday before the scheduled jury trial, Jesse showed up at the jail early in the day to meet with me. He had my friend Sandi with him as his legal assistant, and they were there to begin the preparation process for my testimony before the jury. There was really no doubt that I would have to take the stand in my own defense, given the nature and tragedy of the events. After all, I was the only person who had experienced and lived through all of it and I needed to be ready to tell my story. The three of us sat in the same room for several hours that Friday, then all day Saturday, and all day Sunday until extremely late in the evening.

I still had not, at this point, spoken about most of the abuse, and very little of it in any detail. It was extremely difficult — all that shame, guilt, and pain coming to the surface for the first time in ten years, to be spoken aloud and acknowledged. With it came immeasurable grief, anxiety, discomfort, disgrace, and humiliation. There were times when I became truly angry at Jesse for asking hard questions and pushing me for answers. He made me feel like he was punishing me, even though I knew, deep down, that he was simply doing his job. That feeling of being punished though, was way too close to the feelings of diminishment and belittlement that Paul inflicted, and I lashed out at Jesse more than once through tears and anger. I told him, "Fuck you, Jesse" a couple of times because I saw him sometimes as Paul.

Those three days were long and tiring for all of us, and I cried and acted out many times in fear and trauma. Sandi also broke down in tears more than once — the frustration and agitation in the room was palpable for all of us. By day three, I was feeling overwhelmed and emotionally beat-up. Jesse and Sandi left in a hurry that night, and I am certain they were also feeling overwhelmed and drained themselves. I was distraught at making them feel so awful. I really did not understand my behavior at all.

Looking back, it is clear what happened, but that does not make me feel any better. They put their hearts and souls and time and energy into helping me, and I will be forever grateful and indebted to them. I only hope that they both realize that my disappointing behavior during that time was not intentional or directed towards either of them, but only occurred because of the agonizing ordeal of revealing the truth.

I do remember that on that Sunday, when I was feeling so overwhelmed, I asked Jesse about a possible plea deal. I told him I was not sure I could testify at my trial. It seemed so terrifying and impossible, just the thought of speaking my truth in front of a courtroom of people, including my family and close friends, his family, the press, people associated with the Michigan State Police, and the jury. I knew it was important, but emotionally, mentally, I did not think I was capable of doing it at all.

The next day — which was two days before the scheduled trial date — Jesse informed me that a plea deal was being discussed with the prosecuting attorney. He and Dean had concluded that working towards a plea deal would avoid the unknown elements and outcome of a jury trial. He indicated that the prosecutor was willing to talk sensibly about the facts, as well as any hopes for a fair and just outcome — not only for me as a defendant, but for Paul's family as well. The plea deal was reached based on the extreme extent of the abuse and other facts realized during the investigations — facts pertaining to Paul.

On July 13, 2010, I entered a plea of guilty to Second Degree Murder. The prosecutor would recommend a maximum sentence of 15 years, with a minimum sentence to be determined by the court — the judge in this matter. The court accepted my plea of guilty, and sentencing was scheduled, coincidentally, for August 10, 2010, exactly one year to the day since the tragedy.

* *

I continue to this day to describe the day of the event as a tragedy. Webster defines "tragedy" as: *"a very sad or tragic event or sequence of events; a disaster."* Webster subsequently describes "disaster" as: *"any happening that causes great harm or damage; serious or sudden misfortune; calamity."* I believe the entire term of my relationship with Paul was an extreme misfortune, from the very first minute to the very last minute. I will forever look at what happened as a tragedy — a disastrous tragedy.

With the sentencing date pending, Jesse prepared a Sentencing Memorandum which would be presented to the judge and the prosecuting attorney. This document was incredibly detailed about the events leading up to the date of the crime and included information obtained from the investigation and witness statements. Also attached was the final report from Dr. Barbara Jones-Smith and letters of support from family members, friends, and many of the attorneys that I had worked for over the 28-years of my career. Hundreds of pornographic pictures from Paul's computer were included as well. This document and all of its attachments were filed with the court and are included in my case file.

# CHAPTER 7: SENTENCING

Sentencing began at 10:00 a.m. on the morning of August 10, 2010, and many people were in attendance. My children, my parents, my siblings, and many close friends and family members were there to support me and witness the final decision of the court. Everyone was feeling rather sick. All of my support people sat on one side of the courtroom, behind the defense table, and when there were no more seats available on that side, chairs were lined up in the middle of the aisle. None of the people who loved me wanted to sit on his side of the courtroom behind the prosecuting attorney, so those seats were left empty.

Three of his immediate family members were in attendance and wanted to speak on the record — which is status quo at any sentencing in which the victim has been killed — but only four or five other people sat on that side of the aisle. There were press from television stations and newspaper outlets, and although I heard that State Police people were there, not one of them was present in the courtroom at any time during the sentencing hearing. Apparently, they listened to the proceedings in an adjacent room.

It was an uncommonly long sentencing hearing — longer than any I had heard about in my line of work. Obviously, many hearings had taken place throughout the year as my case pended, but since there had been no trial, much of the discovery was unknown outside of the offices of the prosecutor and the defense. This was the only time when facts and testimony would be spoken about and placed on the court record. The judge, therefore, was willing to venture on the side of leniency when it came to the defense's presentation of my case.

The hearing began with the prosecutor advising the court that three of Paul's family members wanted to speak. The judge agreed to that, however he wanted to take care of some other things first. He stated that he had received several letters on my behalf, some of which were from my own counsel asking for a probationary sentence. I knew that Dean and a couple of other attorneys had suggested that I receive a sentence of probation. Also, a judge I had worked for at District Court wrote, explaining that he had always considered me to be very insecure and seemed to get my feelings hurt easily. The last paragraph of his letter states: "I can only imagine how she might explode one day if she were subjected to years of fear and abuse; physical, sexual, and especially verbal abuse. Her personality makeup is fragile, and she feels things more intensely than most of us do. She needs years of therapy before being released from court supervision. That may be more likely to occur while on a supervised probation than in the bowels of the prison system. Please give this some thought in making your excruciatingly difficult sentencing decision."

The sentencing judge took the time to make certain that I was aware of the fact that I would be going to prison at the time I entered my plea. I assured him that I was well aware of this, and that I understood it. He wanted the record to reflect these important things, and he also wanted it known that the court could not sentence someone convicted of Second Degree Murder to probation under Michigan law. This was completely understood on my part and by my counsel as well.

The Judge also wanted Jesse to know that he had to file his Sentencing Memorandum and accompanying materials as part of the court file, and that it would be open to the public and part of the public record. It would not be sealed because of the pornographic photographs, "even though some people might consider them repugnant or morally outrageous", the judge declared on the record.

Once these things were taken care of on the record, it was time for Paul's family members to speak. His brother spoke first, then his mother, followed by his only sister. They all blamed me for what had happened, and all three of them were convinced that I was a liar. They did not believe that Paul had ever mistreated me, and they could not believe that the word "torture" was being used to describe any of his actions towards me. His brother was particularly offended by that term and stated to the court that their father had taught all four sons to never mistreat or raise a hand to a woman, ever. His brother felt certain that Paul's character had been shaped by their father, as his own had been growing up. He did not believe Paul had ever hit me or abused me physically. When Paul's mother stood up and took the podium, it was evident that her hate and contempt for me was overwhelming. I understood this completely, and I hurt for her and all of his siblings for not only what I did to him, but also for what they were about to learn about Paul himself. They will never forgive me, of this I am certain, but I do not have the strength to dwell on that fact. Some of the things Paul's mother said at my sentencing hearing:

> "I cannot put into words what you have done to my family and me. Our whole family is still trying to come to some kind of understanding of what you were thinking of or hoping to achieve with that heinous act. You will have to live with all you have done to my family, and to your parents, your siblings, and your children and grandbabies. I'm sure Chad will have nightmares for what you did to him. Plus, your daughter and granddaughters will only get to see you through bars. That is if they

come to see you at all. You have brought this on all by yourself. You have smeared my husband's name, my son's name, and my grandson's name. And I am so pleased you will be receiving your dues. Only if I had my way, you would never see the light of day again without bars." End of testimony.

This is not the end of what she said, but it is the bulk of her statement. Her comment about the family name being smeared is because her husband was Melvin Paul Holbrook, Jr., my husband was Melvin Paul Holbrook III, and his son with Starr is Melvin Paul Holbrook, IV.

His sister was the last one to stand up, and she spoke about me blaming her brother for what I had done. Her brother had done nothing, she said, and my lying needed to stop. She said that I used lies as an excuse for killing him, and she said that she can only conclude that I am a sociopath. Both she and her mother spoke to the court about how they had seen me argue with him, scream at him, and treat him badly while he would sit quietly, saying nothing, simply "taking it."

They both also reported that Paul had told them that I had "cleaned out" our bank accounts, and how he was always having to "bail me out financially." The following is a small portion of what his sister stated to the court:

"In my opinion, the only person abused in this relationship was my brother. You abused him financially, you abused him emotionally by jerking him around on a chain going in and out of that house, using that over him to get him to do what you wanted and pay your bills off. You abused him verbally as well. But he always took you back. And I asked him countless times "why do you put up with this? Why do you go back to her? And he always said the same thing to me, he said 'sis, I love her. I want to take care of her. She needs someone to help her." End of testimony.

I am not going to address these accusations. I have told my story. But it is absolutely true that I needed help. He was right when he told his sister that I needed help, but not the kind of help he gave me.

Following the statements from Paul's family, the judge asked Jesse if he wanted to make a statement on my behalf before the Court passed sentencing. He did, indeed. And Jesse was awesome.

At the beginning, he was apologetic to Paul's family. He said, "First I'd like to address the decedent's family. I'm going to be talking about things that you probably don't know about, and don't want to know about. And they're going to be harsh, and they're going to be hurtful. And I'm apologizing to you up front. I don't do this to hurt you. But there's an important truth that needs to be told, and it's been a dirty secret for a long time." He went on to speak about justice and how he hoped a sentence in a case like mine means something and represents something.

Then, he told the court about Paul's affair with "AC," and read a statement from her. "AC" described her feeling that Paul was extremely controlling in both his demeanor and physical presence. She stated that he came across as over-confident, possibly to compensate for feeling otherwise in reality. "AC" also said that when it came to his personality, Paul was like a Dr. Jekyll and Mr. Hyde. She stated that his behavior had begun to affect her emotionally, and described how she went to her supervisor at the State Police Post where she worked, and that the supervisor had contacted Paul's supervisor requesting that he "cease all contact" with "AC."

Jesse then talked about Starr and read excerpts from her statements into the court record. He also explained the shooting incident — when Starr shot at Paul, initially intending to kill him. He also touched on the fact that there seemed to be a "non-investigation" into that incident by any police agency, let alone the Michigan State Police. Please believe me when I tell you how often I have thought about that during my time here in prison.

Jesse brought forth many important points in his statement to the court. For one, about how everyone who frequented our house knew that Paul's service weapon was not only in reach, but always loaded and "ready to go, just point and shoot." He read into the court record most of each of the letters that Paul sent to me the last time I left him — the ones begging and pleading with me to return to him and his promises to stop the abusive behaviors.

Then, he played an audio tape that he had recorded earlier. It came from a time when he had arrived at the jail extremely late in the evening. It was almost midnight when the officer took me into the library room to meet with him. Jesse explained that he wanted to talk about and, in a sense, reenact the first time Paul raped me. I had come to trust Jesse during our time together, and though I did not know anything about his personal life, I felt that he was sincere, caring, kind and trustworthy; both as a man and as a professional. Jesse explained that he was, in no way, trying to hurt me. Rather, he wanted to try and bring out some of my hidden feelings. He wanted to get some true emotions from me, if possible. He said he felt that the exercise would invoke real feelings of pain and trauma and may take me back to the actual incident. I had told him, in extreme detail, about the first time Paul raped me. But talking about it with words was one thing, reliving it in real time was something else. In that moment, though, I trusted him and said I was willing to do what he asked.

Jesse held his small dictation recorder and explained that he wanted to get my words and reactions on tape. He began by positioning me on top of a table in the jail library. However, the officers working that night were concerned about what was happening and confronted Jesse, questioning his actions. Jesse managed to convince them that he was simply trying to help me, albeit in a very unconventional sort of way. He convinced them that these actions were necessary and within his scope as my counsel. Although I was also hesitant, I assured the officers that I was okay and asked them to please allow him to continue. After that, Jesse had me lie on the floor. He straddled my body, hovering on top of me. He kept saying, "Then what did he do?" "Then what?" "Like this?" I remember directing him with words as this occurred, but I really do not recall much until the end. I remember getting back on my feet, shaking, and crying, then hitting him over and over while repeating, "I hate you. I hate you." Not only had the true emotions of horror and fear come to the surface, but the anger that I had felt for Paul — the anger that I had shoved down over and over for so many years — was suddenly palpable. I was able to feel that, see that, and act on it. Jesse had accomplished what he had set out to do, and I thank him for that. I believe that his "exercise" helped unlock and open the heavy door I had placed on top of that pit of hell. Jesse played the audio tape at my sentencing.

Some of Jesse's further comments from the sentencing transcript, including his closing remarks to the court are included below. In the first part, he speaks about Paul's computer usage.

> "When you look at his private computer, his secret computer, and you go through these pictures, these picture (sic) of evil, these pictures of people crying, these pictures of people being sodomized, poked, made to bleed, made to cry, made to hurt. This is what he was obsessed with, and this is what Joni lived with, and this is what Joni hid from everyone - from both families. Joni went back to him after he

raped her, after he hurt her, because he played on her emotional side with the Lord, and he promised her this would really end. And he knew that she wanted this relationship to work, and he knew she wanted this marriage to work. And he also knew that she did not want to look like a failure again. He played it up quite will (sic). Poor me. My wife is just some crazy, in his words, bitch. And he would tell everyone at church, his coworkers, 'she's just crazy, you know, I'm just taking care of her,' yet he's the puppet master back at the house pulling the strings and tormenting her. And we think to ourselves, how could she shoot him, though? Why couldn't she leave? Well, she did leave. She left three times. And three times he tricked her back into that trap. So here we are today, she shot him in his sleep, shot him in his bed, three bullets, shot him with his own gun, ironically the gun that he adamantly would tell her "it's loaded, the safety is off, all you got (sic) to do is pull the trigger.' Joni never touched a gun in her life until that night. Joni had never fired a gun. Joni wouldn't know how to load a gun. Joni wouldn't know how to put the safety on, take the safety off. Joni wouldn't know how to do any of that. But ironically, she pulled the trigger of the very gun that he always told her "it's loaded, all you got (sic) to do it pull the trigger.' The very gun that the doctors from Forest View called and told him to keep away from her, the very gun that his own coworkers suggested to him it might be a better idea not to bring it home. Now, here we are, we're Americans, and we're proud to be Americans. And what do we do as Americans? We preemptively strike out. We kill in the name of fear, in the name of terror. We send missiles into Iraq. We send missiles into Afghanistan. Innocent people die. Not so innocent people die. But nonetheless, we're comfortable with the concept. We're very comfortable with preemptively killing to protect ourselves. We all go to bed every night not worrying about it, not thinking about it. And we think our actions as Americans are justified to kill others to protect ourselves. Well, Paul trapped Joni and pushed her, and pushed her, and pushed her, and put her in a corner. And what did she do? She had two choices, to either be killed or kill. And she killed him because she truly believed - - truly believed - - that he was going to kill her one day. And when you look at the path of violence and where this was going, she had every right and reason to think that. This man threatened her life. He was a big guy. He was bigger than me. He'd stand in her path, wouldn'tt let her pass through the door. 'Sit the fuck down. Sit the fuck down. You're not going anywhere.' And he'd make her sit there - - just sit there. And he'd stand there. 'Okay, now you can leave.' He'd come in the house and slam the door. He'd whip the shit off the counter. He'd punch the refrigerator so hard that he put his knuckles in the refrigerator in front of her. He'd smash the cabinets until his knuckles would bleed. So here we are today passing judgment on what happened here. But the truth is she had no choice. She had to shoot him in his sleep because he would have killed her if she triggered that anger, if she triggered that rage that he held so close, rarely showed, but held, and if she triggered that she would have had only one time, one chance to do that, and he would have bludgeoned her to death as he told her he would. So, when we pass sentence on her, let us think about what happened here. This wasn't an innocent victim. This was a man who tormented women throughout his life. This was a man who

- - this was a man who was very intelligent and manipulating and controlling, who knew what to do. So yes, she did shoot him. And yes, it is horrible. And from a human standpoint, I do sympathize and understand the anger and hatred that the decedent's family holds toward her, but please let's look at the truth, the truth of what happened here and where we ended up. This nightmare started 23 years ago when his first wife shot at him. And had that been addressed properly and professionally, possibly we wouldn't be here today. Your Honor, when you sentence my client this morning - - or this afternoon - - I plead to you to give her a sentence of fairness that incorporates everything that happened and lead up to this. This Court had (sic) been more than fair during these proceedings, and I don't think that she would be in this position she's in right now had this been in another court, in front of another judge. And I pray that this court can allow the likes of justice to shine through here and give her a sentence that's appropriate. She's been punished enough. She's lived through a hell. She's been in prison for a long time." End of Jesse's statement to the Court.

One of the last presentations was really kind of unusual at a sentencing — the judge allowed Jesse to call some of my family members to take the witness stand, be sworn in, and answer pointed questions pertaining to my relationship with Paul — things they had observed and what they were aware of in our relationship. My daughter Ashley, my son Chad, my sister Debra and two people I had worked with and knew well, all testified. Each one of them was stoic and thoughtful, and Jesse's questions gave the court a glimpse into what people outside of the marriage had observed, along with their thoughts about Paul himself. I am so proud of both of my children and my sister for their strength to sit on that witness stand and speak about the situation. I am beyond blessed that each one of my loved ones support and stand behind me to this very day.

Finally, the Court gave me an opportunity to speak my thoughts, which I did. I apologized to each one of his family members individually, and I did the best I could to explain why I had killed him, even though I am sure they will never understand my thought process. After all of the years that have passed, I can say with certainty that I, myself, still do not completely understand my thought process, but I know exactly what pushed me to make the decision.

It was time for the Judge to speak and pass sentence. He had asked the Prosecuting Attorney if "the People wanted to be heard on sentencing?" The prosecutor's response was simply "No, your Honor, I don't think I can ...." That was it. He did not speak another word or cross-examine any of the witnesses. I am sure that it would have been allowed, but he chose to remain silent. The judge, on the other hand, had many things to say. I am including most of it. The Honorable James M. Batzer said:

> "Before the Court for sentencing is a woman 48 years of age, the Defendant, Joni K Holbrook, and she is here on her plea of guilty to the offense of second-degree murder. And the circumstances of the offense, the immediate circumstances of the offense are that something (sic) around 1:00 in the morning, a year ago today, it turns out, the Defendant told the Court at the plea taking that she had gotten out of bed, was - - the deceased, her husband, was asleep, and she had sat up for about 20 minutes thinking about it, and she was certainly upset and angry, and she went out into the - - into his vehicle, and located the deceased's service - - I think she said revolver but I think it was a semi-automatic handgun, and

went back in and shot him to death. She shot him three times, including in the head. And then she called the police.

His family wonders why there was a plea to second-degree murder, and why it was there was prosecutor's recommendation for a maximum sentence of 15 years. They may not be the only ones who wonder why, but I'll try and explain it. I did not negotiate the plea, but I think that I do understand it. There is (sic) a case in Oakland County not all that long ago. This woman had been a schoolteacher. And she was liked by everyone, her students, and she went to a hardware store, bought some kind of hatchet, and her husband was out in the garage, I believe, and she went up behind him and hit him with the hatchet and killed him. She went to trial. She was convicted of first-degree murder. The trial judge was very moved by the evidence of how she had been abused for years - - for years. And the trial judge set aside the first-degree murder conviction, relying on some law that the Court thought applied. And the Michigan Court of Appeals overturned it, said essentially to the Circuit judge, you can't do that, the jury said first-degree murder, and it's first-degree murder, and that means the sentence in Michigan for first-degree murder is life in prison without parole. So, if you are convicted of first-degree murder in Michigan, you will never get out of prison. You're going to die in prison unless the Governor of the State, who has that authority, commutes the sentence.

Mr. Robb, able - - highly able - - attorney that he is, he has been around a long time. Mr. Robb remembers trying a case - - was it Grayling or Gaylord?

Mr. Robb: Gaylord.

The Court: What was the case?

Mr. Robb: A woman was charged with open murder, similar to the charges here, and we hired a psychologist who testified for the first time in Michigan about the Battered Wife Syndrome, of how an abused woman, person, eventually will break and strike back. And in my letter to you, I was - - I was - - I think the abuse that this woman suffered was far greater than what Jeanette Smith suffered, but -

The Court: What was the -

Mr. Robb: We did not have the law on our side in this case. And what needs to be changed is the law. It is not right.

The Court: What was the verdict?

Mr. Robb: Not guilty.

The Court: All right.

Mr. Robb: She was found not guilty.

The Court: So, there you have it. Oakland County first-degree murder, never, ever get out of prison. Gaylord, a jury verdict of not guilty, acquittal.

So, the prosecutor and the defense are between the proverbial rock and a hard place in this case. The defendant thinks they've got many - - many things - - you've heard some of it today, you haven't heard all details - but the defense thinks they can get a lot of this into evidence and run what's called a battered spouse defense. And in Michigan, under the law, that's self- defense (sic). And they've got a decent chance at an acquittal. Maybe more than a decent chance. Maybe not so much as they'd like. And the risk is she gets convicted of first-degree murder, she never gets out of prison.

The prosecutor's got a case where she sits down for about 20 minutes thinking about it, which is evidence of premeditation and deliberation. She deliberately goes out to the car, she knows where the gun is, but the prosecutor knows that all of this - all of these things that you've heard about here a bit today are going to be brought out. And a jury can certainly hear that evidence, and decide to acquit, to decide to convict of something less than the first-degree murder. In this kind of case, I would give the jury the option of - - I'd give them the option of manslaughter as well. So, this agreement represents a compromise from both sides on the risks of trial. And what is the 15 year cap? That's the maximum possible prison sentence in Michigan for manslaughter. This is, in many respects, a plea to the offense - a plea of guilty to the offense of manslaughter, although it's not called that. It's called second-degree murder, but the cap on the sentence is the same as a manslaughter.

Well, there's a rule in law. It's been around the common law for a long time. It's the law in Michigan. It's called the rule of provocation. And I'm not telling the attorneys anything they don't know here. But the rule of provocation says if there's a killing that happens, an intentional killing even, but it happens in circumstances where the killer is acting out of overwhelming passion before there's been time to cool down, than (sic) what would otherwise be murder is not murder at all, it's manslaughter. And the classic situation for the rule of provocation is the man comes home, walks in on his wife having sex with another man, and kills him and maybe her too, but it's the man catching them in flagrante delicto, it's called. So, it is a rule that really came out of circumstances to protect males, because we all know men get angry when they encounter that kind of situation. And they get so angry, they kill. And it's not murder.

Well, this defendant here was so angry - was so angry - she killed her husband. But the anger wasn't the anger of the moment that where if she walked away for a few minutes, for a few hours, for a few days, the anger, the passion would dissipate, and cooler heads would prevail. This defendant, this woman, has been seething with anger for years. And whatever it is about her personality, I've gotten all kinds of letters. I've gotten letters from the family of Sergeant Holbrook who was killed. I've gotten letters from friends and family of people who worked - people who the defendant worked for. And everyone sees this - everyone sees the defendant, and uniformly, in a way that says, well, she was nice, we liked her, but she is not assertive. She's not (sic) assertive person. She's someone who isn't self-confident. And so, she never had the wherewithal - although I recognize that one of the deceased's family members has said she is (sic) seen the defendant angry at Sergeant Holbrook and standing up to him. But they say about the defendant, she doesn't have the wherewithal to be assertive. Either she's so - that's part of her personality, or she was so ground down she didn't know how anymore. But more likely she never was very assertive. And so, she is engaged in, over a number of years, in doing things that were violative of her sense of self, sense of self-worth, sense of dignity, values, whatever.

I recognize there's some people in the world who wouldn't be bothered by any of it, most of it, but it wasn't for her. And this just went on, and resulted in this horrible, horrible tragedy.

There is nothing that this Court can do in the way of sentencing that's going to make it satisfactory to the people here who are aligned with one side or the other. There's no answer. There's no answer to the - to Sergeant Holbrook's loss of life in the sentence this Court imposes. There's no answer to the pain of the defendant's family in any sentence this Court imposes. The law is an imperfect vehicle, but it's what we have. And this defendant on her plea, in the eyes of the law, is guilty of second-degree murder. And it's a compromise. But I'm treating it very closely to and akin to a manslaughter. I will observe this. If I accept everything that was said here today about the things that happened to Joni Holbrook, things that - the activities of her husband - as true, and it's coming from many sources, she had - this defendant had many opportunities to walk away, to get away, to stay away. There were two separations. Plus, there were her suicide attempts - I think there were two. One - but where she was hospitalized. I think there's something about her personality, maybe something in the relationship, she did not have the wherewithal to do that. Now, there's a school of thought in psychology, people who study in the so-called battered spouse syndrome - and I'm using that loosely - that says victims of this become, in essence, paralyzed, and can't act, which is to say people no longer have a choice. I think there were opportunities for her to act. She didn't.

It is the sentence of the Court that the defendant be committed to the custody of the Michigan Department of Corrections for a minimum term of not more than six years and a maximum term of not more than 15 years. Now under Michigan's indeterminate sentencing law, the Court does not decide when she gets out other than the law is that she has to serve the minimum term. After that, it is up to the Parole Board, which is part of the Department of Corrections, whether she gets out at the minimum or serves more than that or serves - - or serves the maximum.

I know that this sentence is going to be unsatisfactory to parties aligned on both sides. But I think this plea was a compromised plea. It was a rational compromise. It was a rational compromise by both sides. And the Court's sentence recognizes that compromise, and it is itself a compromise between the competing elements of this case that argue for leniency form (sic) one point of view, and that argue for harshness and severity from (sic) another point of view." End of Judge Batzer's statement.

So, it was over. I was immediately handcuffed and taken out of the courtroom. I was not able to speak to any of my family members, and although all of them had come to the jail to see me over the past year's time, those visits were had with a large piece of plexiglass between us while we conversed on a telephone receiver. Exactly like what you see in the movies — just like that. I had not been able to touch or hug my children, my parents, or anyone else in my family for the entire year, and although my attorneys requested that I be able to have a final, sit-down-in-the-same-room meeting with my family, that request was denied. On the evening of the sentencing, at about 8:30 in the evening, Dean and Jesse showed up back at the jail to see me one last time. They had left following the sentencing and joined my family and my friends, at the request of my father, at a local restaurant to have a bite to eat and a cocktail or two, and their spirits were high when they told me how much fun they had spending time with my loved ones. I was jealous, of course, but very happy that they were all able to spend some time together while bringing the entire hard work on my case to an end, with everyone feeling a sense of relief and gratitude with the final outcome.

I was transferred to the Women's Huron Valley Correctional Facility on August 12, 2010, to begin my sentence. The judge gave me credit for all 276 days that I had spent in the county jail. My first possible release date would be November 6, 2015.

Yes, I am in prison, but in many respects, I am freer now than I was at home in my own house with my own husband.

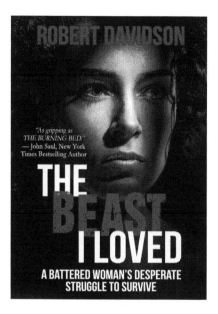

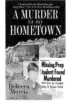